JANE PACKER'S
NEW FLOWER
ARRANGING

JANE PACKER'S
NEW FLOWER ARRANGING

TEXT BY JANE PACKER AND LOUISE SIMPSON

PHOTOGRAPHY BY PETER WILLIAMS

conran
OCTOPUS

For my 'Boys': Gary, Rebby & Ted.

AUTHOR'S ACKNOWLEDGEMENTS

I embarked upon this book with a certain amount of trepidation, but finding myself surrounded by such a talented team instilled me with a great confidence and enabled me to enjoy the project.
My sincere thanks go to: Peter Williams, who, with his tireless patience in the search for perfection, created such wonderful photography; Róisín Nield whose attention to detail, colour and texture guaranteed wonderful 'environments' for my flowers; Louise Simpson, who made sense of my jumbled thoughts and rambles, adding her own polish and professionalism; Georgina and the entire team at Conran Octopus, who made this book happen; and finally my thanks to Cappy, Dean, Donna, Mark, Michelle and Sam, whose hard work and support allowed me time to work on this exciting project.

First published in 1994 by Conran Octopus Limited,
37 Shelton Street, London WC2H 9HN
Reprinted 1994, 1995
Original designs and flower arrangements © Jane Packer 1994
Text copyright © Conran Octopus 1994
Design and layout copyright © Conran Octopus 1994
Photography copyright © Peter Williams 1994

Project Editor
LOUISE SIMPSON

Art Editor and Designer
GEORGINA RHODES

Photographer
PETER WILLIAMS

Stylist
RÓISÍN NIELD

Editor
BARBARA MELLOR

Editorial Assistant
JANE CHAPMAN

Production Controller
JULIA GOLDING

A CIP record for this book is available from the British Library
ISBN 1-85029-980-3
Typeset by Richard Proctor
Printed in China

CONTENTS

FOREWORD

This is a book for all flower lovers – not just the habitual flower arranger, but everyone who loves buying flowers from the local florist or picking them from the garden to put in a vase and decorate their home. In fact, most people today are rather against flower arranging. The vogue is for flowers that look natural and un-arranged. And I couldn't agree more with that senti-ment! The days of flower arranging by prescription are long over and today we prefer to go for what looks as if it has come straight from the garden rather than the evening class. Your tried and tested method of ar-ranging may be to swoosh your favourite flowers into the nearest vase, ruffle up the blooms with another deft wrist movement and then sit back with a sigh. Yet this approach can seem unsatisfactory in time, as it is all too tempting to use the same flowers, plonk them in the nearest vase, and end up with a rather stiff bundle. Often you may simply need the confidence to search out unusual varieties, use a wider selection of foliage, or experiment with less obvious containers.

Here then are a few personal suggestions for flower combinations, designs and containers to prompt you to become that little bit more adventurous, creative and, dare I say, distinctive. Some of the arrangements, such as the red pepper bush or the anemone tree, may inspire you to try a different style of table arrangement, or encourage you to decorate your home in an extra special way – the classical ivy wreath, for instance, is a Christmas decoration that is as effective as it is simple to make. Here I have included a few basic rules that will help you find your feet, such as how to prolong the life of flowers, support stems in a vase, and make the few

PREVIOUS PAGE
Enamel jugs and galvanized buckets and troughs containing eucalyptus, sea holly and poppy seedheads.

precious blooms you have bought or nurtured go further than you would think possible.

I have also decided to arrange the flowers seasonally rather than by occasion. This is not only because it is more practical, but I am a firm advocate of using native European flowers whenever possible, rather than ex-pensive exotic or forced blooms. Vita Sackville-West once said, when asked to name her favourite flower 'Any flower, turn by turn, which happens to be in season at the moment'. This encapsulates my own attitude to flowers, and I think that seasonal arranging is not only more satisfying, but also encourages you to ring the changes and try out different foliage or flowers as the seasons roll on. A vase of hawthorn berries and chestnut leaves in the autumn is so much more satis-fying than those sad forced tulips, whose anaemic blo-oms wilt as soon as you take them out of their paper.

In addition to seasonal favourites, I have also tried to provide ideas for grouping some of the many more unusual flowers that are readily available today – such as echinops, arum lilies, sunflowers and fennel. These have all been around for years but have somehow been neglected in favour of the obligatory carnations and gypsophila so beloved by the high-street florist. Be bold and try out the unfamiliar from time to time. You may well be pleasantly surprised and you will always learn a little more about flowers by experimenting.

On a final note, I think it is important to stress that the arrangements I have chosen are really intended to be inspirational ideas rather than projects to be copied precisely. Whether they serve to provoke a little lateral thinking, bring depth to the 'swoosh' approach or provide purely visual pleasure – as Peter Williams' magical, moody photography cannot fail to do – I hope ultimately that this book will increase your love and understanding of flowers.   **JANE PACKER**

INTRODUCTION

The equipment you need for flower arranging need not be complicated, expensive or bulky. This really is one of the joys of working with flowers – once you have made your selection, it takes no time at all to trim the stems and plunge them into cool water. Yet there are a few basic techniques and some types of containers that may get your display off to a good start.

CONTAINERS

Most of us have a very open mind when it comes to choosing what to put flowers in – a container these days is as likely to be a Perrier bottle, a metal bucket or an enamel jug as a traditional flower vase. In fact, anything that holds water and enhances your flowers will do. I am a particular fan of grouped containers, as you will soon see, especially when I can get hold of unusual vessels that work well together. Sometimes I look for shape, sometimes colour. Enamel is a particular favourite, and my collection of enamel jugs, gleaned from second-hand shops, is ever increasing. Limpid, translucent glass will always be a winner – especially with flowers that have interesting or graceful stems – and the great interest in recycled glass has filled the shops with every shade under the sun – from palest blue to deep amber. With glass, you have the additional interest of being able to see the stems under water, and on page 28 I have suggested ideas for filling the same glass tank so that the arrangement is as interesting below the rim as it is above.

Terracotta is another material that has been revived, revamped and reappraised in the last few years. Pots that once belonged only in the greenhouse have stolen their way into many a cottagey or informal room. Terracotta is porous, and therein lies its delight and its downfall: the surface that allows wonderful fungal blooms to develop in the garden also spreads water over your table top. If you are worried about the surface beneath a terracotta pot, always place it on a non-porous mat or use a glazed terracotta saucer. Alternatively, you can seal terracotta with a coat of acrylic varnish or simply line your vessel with polythene. The Shaker pots of wheat (page 14) are simple terracotta flowerpots, which I have painted with oil-based paint and decorated with a strip of matching gingham fabric. This is cheap, fun and easy to do.

There is also a legion of baskets, boxes, vases and jugs on the market these days, and the choice is entirely up to you: weathered wooden trugs, baskets made from moss, bracken or leaves, and hand-painted items are just some of the possibilities. Some of the most effective containers are simply biscuit tins, old teapots, galvanized metal buckets and even chipped or cracked vases. In fact I think the older the vessel the nicer it is. If you are worried about water leaking out of a crack in a vase, just put a smaller watertight container inside it.

HEIGHT AND COLOUR

There are no particular rules about which size flowers should go in which containers. However, one useful tip is to make your arrangement about one and a half times the height of your vessel. Don't be intimidated by this rule, just bear it in mind as a starting point. It should also be stressed that flower stems may often look best if cut down quite severely. In fact some of the tallest and most imposing blooms can be cut down further than most people would dare. I often trim amaryllis right down to suit a table arrangement, and its audacious trumpet blooms look stunning when seen from above. Suitability of container depends so much on the environment you are decorating. In a modern, minimalist living room, longiflorum lilies might look best in an elongated white vase; the same flowers in a more

Old country jugs are some of my favourite containers for informal arrangements.

countrified room will work in a rounded terracotta jug, matched with soft, variegated foliage.

I don't favour particular colour rules either. Common sense and individual taste are your two instinctive guides. If you are using a patterned container, make sure that it ties in in some way with your flowers: a strongly patterned red diamond container with graphic red tulips for instance, or a faded pastel vase with a bunch of butterfly sweet peas. Similarly, match darker, textured material with the richer flowers of winter and autumn, and try lighter, more delicate vessels for the warmer months – a burnished deep bronze container will set off polished winter holly and scarlet azaleas, while a white porcelain vase may be more appropriate for apricot roses and honeysuckle. In other words, make a visual link between the colour, mood or shape of your plant material and the container.

CONTAINER WIDTH

The width of your container mouth is as important, if not more so, than the shape or colour of the vessel you have chosen. A bulbous vase which looks capacious but has a narrow mouth will only work with slender stemmed but generously petalled flowers, such as sweet peas. A narrow vase with a wide mouth will present different problems, not least of which will be that your flowers will just slide to one side of it. There are, however, a few ways of anchoring your flowers in a vase that is effectively too wide. Florist's foam and pin holders are the most obvious way, but these mechanics can end up producing an effect that looks stiff and unnatural. Another simpler method is to use a grid of clear adhesive tape stuck in a lattice across the mouth of the vase. The lattice holds the flowers gently, and prevents them flopping in disarray over the edge. This is a particularly useful tip when you have only a few

expensive blooms to hand, and it instantly makes them look like a much more generous bunch. The more conventional forms of mechanics – chicken wire, floral foam and pins – will always have a place in formal flower arranging, but it does take practice and time to work with them effectively.

Another way of making a wide container more versatile is to place a small vessel inside it to hold the water. This is particularly useful for baskets, where the mouth is usually enormous and flowers need more support than the wicker allows. Flowers that have particularly delicate stems, such as pansies and violets, also benefit from being fixed in an inner container, which is narrow enough to hold them securely. Their delicate stems would not work with florist's foam or a pin holder.

CHOOSING PLANT MATERIAL

Always buy flowers that are partly in bud if you want them to last a long time. The tighter the bud, the longer the flowers will last. However, if the bud is completely green the flower may never open. Spring flowers, especially daffodils, are particularly likely to disappoint in this way. If you want your flowers to be at their best on the day that you buy them, then you can be more daring and go for flowers that are almost fully opened.

Before buying any flower, always check the condition of the leaves and the petals; if either look brown or discoloured, leave well alone. If stems have been stripped of leaves, it may be a sign of the florist trying to disguise a dying bunch. Flowers that are wrapped in cellophane should be scrutinized for signs of botrytis or mildew. Always peel back the cellophane and make sure it is not the only thing keeping the flowers in bud. Some flowers may look deceptively mature when they are in fact just opening. Stocks often look crumpled and

Shaker pots – plain sheaves of wheat arranged in two colourful painted terracotta pots. The arrangement derives its effect from symmetrical simplicity.

crinkled in bud, but unless they are also brown and mushy, this is a sign of freshness. Be careful with carnations, however. If you can see their white stamens and the petals are curling inwards, they are over.

However enticing wild flowers, never be tempted to pick them. As well as the damage you may be doing to the environment by removing potentially threatened species, you are actually breaking the law. And on a final note, if you are picking flowers or foliage yourself, be careful with berries. Many are poisonous, and of course irresistible to small children.

CONDITIONING FLOWERS

When you unwrap your flowers or foliage, immediately trim off a good inch from the bottom of each stem at an angle – this exposes the largest amount of surface area for taking up water. Then plunge the stems into clear, fresh water for at least an hour before arranging. See page 48 for special treatment for roses. I never bother with sugar in the water, or aspirin, but flower food (the sachets you often get with a bouquet) is effective as it contains both food and an anti-bacterial substance to prolong life. For a homemade anti-bacterial remedy, add a teaspoon of household bleach to a litre of water. This should keep the flowers in fine petal for longer.

When you are ready to arrange the flowers, you need to trim off any leaves that will be below the water line of the vase. Put the water in the vase first, and then add the flowers and foliage. I tend to remove the outer leaves of tulips as they flop anyway, but I always prefer roses with as many of their leaves left on as possible.

Water should also be renewed on a daily basis; this may sound like a fuss, but all you need to do is to put the vase – with the arrangement intact – under the tap, and run the water in gently at the side until the rim overflows. This leaves the flowers undisturbed.

EQUIPMENT

There is not a great deal you need for informal flower arranging. If you want to make swags and wreaths, you need a few pieces of structural equipment (called mechanics in the trade), such as florist's foam, chicken wire and wreath frames. Here is a brief resumé of some of the things I use, but don't regard this as a shopping list. You may manage with just a good selection of vases and a pair of secateurs.

CUTTING

Whether you prefer using a large pair of kitchen scissors, a knife or a pair of secateurs, choose something that works well, is sharp and will cope with tough and thick stems but will not damage delicate ones.

BINDING

I use green twine to bind stems together. Good old hairy string is also excellent when you want a textural effect. I also use raffia for finishing off topiary, and ribbons and gold twine for wreaths and swags.

SUPPORTING

Florist's foam is essential for making more formal arrangments – from small table displays to large church pedestals. *Grey foam* is hard and brittle and used for dried flowers. *Green foam* is water-retaining and used for fresh flowers.

Adhesive tape – I often make a lattice work of adhesive tape to support the necks of some flowers (see page 56). It is a very quick, simple method and has the added advantage of being invisible.

Chicken wire holds stems firmly at the bottom of containers. It can also be moulded into a special shape and filled with moss or foam. Obviously, it is better not to use chicken wire in transparent containers.

WIRES AND ADHESIVES

There are many types of wire available in dozens of lengths and thicknesses. Generally, a medium gauge stub wire is useful for wiring swags and for topiary. You need a thinner wire for wiring individual flower heads. Florist's tape is useful for holding down foam or chicken wire, as it is strong and waterproof. A glue gun is more specialized and not essential – it is used for large-scale arrangements on the whole, when dried materials or fruits need to be fixed quickly to a swag or wreath.

MOSS

Florists use moss like builders use cement. It binds together flowers, covers ugly wire or foam and finishes off arrangements with a natural flourish. There are many kinds of moss, but the following four are the most useful and can be purchased from florists:

Spanish moss, tends to be expensive as it is imported. Use it sparingly as a decorative, hanging moss.

Lichen, also known as reindeer moss, this is sold in its dry form, and its silvery-grey texture is used for enhancing the surface of an arrangement or a topiary.

Carpet moss, is bright green and velvety in texture and useful as a surface moss. (It is very like *bun moss* which grows in rounded clumps.)

Sphagnum moss, this is a tendrilly moss that holds water like a sponge and supports flower stems. Use it for filling wreaths or as a surface layer on arrangements. Spray sphagnum regularly to top up its water reservoir.

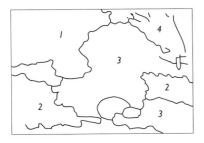

1 spanish moss
2 lichen
3 carpet moss
4 sphagnum moss

SPRING

SPRING FLOWERS

For most of us, spring is the season for making new resolutions, sorting out the paraphenalia of our lives and trying to achieve a sense of calm order after the excesses of the Christmas period.

Just as we have packed away the Christmas lights, we are now more than ready to set aside the reds and dark greens of winter and shake out the new pastels, chartreuse greens and blues of spring. The palette is so fresh and inviting that we are momentarily stunned by its profusion. Pale yellow is perhaps the quintessential colour of spring – with masses of primroses and narcissi all displaying this beautiful buttermilk hue. It is com-plemented by all the blues of spring – the delft blue of hyacinths, the deep violets of primulas and the azures of irises and scillas.

First on offer is of course the fresh and ever-appealing daffodil. Bunches have probably been displayed in the shops throughout the winter, but the spring daffodil is brighter and cheaper than its forced winter counter-part. You can afford to buy several bunches and mass them together in a profusion of heady scent and glowing colour. Narcissi are especially fragrant, look out for varieties such as 'Cheerfulness', and small pots of these are very pretty around the house.

Tulips are also in abundant supply – with broad petals of darkest red, deep purple, pale yellow and fresh white. With their strong lines, simple shapes and intense colours, tulips always look good on their own, in a simple elegant vase. Even when they begin to fade and their translucent petals peel away from their dark core, they have a dignity and beauty all of their own.

There is also a glorious array of miniature bulbs for potted-up displays in the house – such as the dwarf irises, grape hyacinths, crocuses, snowdrops and miniature tulips – and their delicate structures and markings are best appreciated really close up.

*I irises **2** Icelandic poppies **3** parrot tulips **4** double tulips **5** grape hyacinths **6** narcissi **7** snowdrops*

SPRING FOLIAGE

In the early spring, you really have little more foliage at your disposal than you did in the winter. However, as you start to look around you, you begin to notice small buds sprouting out of gnarled brown twigs – scaley sticky buds protecting the first green shoots or small lime-green catkins dangling from otherwise barren twigs. A few of these branches will offset pale yellow narcissi or flowering rhododendrons to dramatic effect. Then there is always pussy willow, which with its sparse, graphic branches spattered with buds of palest grey cashmere, is synonymous with early spring. It is both long lasting and beautiful when cut, and although frequently paired with daffodils and other spring bulbs, its has the sparse graphic quality that looks truly striking on its own. Broom and forsythia are other linear spring shrubs, spangled with their starry yellow flowers, which make interesting and colourful components in modern arrangements.

Later in the spring, foliage begins to unfurl at a furious rate, peeling back from resiny wrappings or bursting out of hairy mantles. Sprays of horse chestnut, shimmering with pale white candles of flowers, deck the roadside, whilst country lanes begin to undulate with the first stems of cow parsley, or Queen Anne's lace, as it is

more poetically known. Towards the end of April, there will be the added excitement of Solomon's seal, lily of the valley and tender honeysuckle.

Many of the pale green young leaves of trees, such as silver birch, beech, and chestnut, work well with spring flowers, whilst green shrubs such as skimmia and mahonia are also very versatile for arranging. Spring flowers may provide sufficient greenery in themselves: the fleshy green leaves of primulas, daffodils and hyacinths provide plenty of colour contrast to the flowers, whilst sprays of fruit bloom really need no other foil than their own green or bronzed leaves.

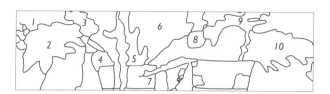

1 pussy willow (salix) *2 choisya 3 pear blossom 4 birch catkin* (betula) *5 eucalyptus 6 elaeagnus 7 larch 8 camellia 9 mahonia 10 euphorbia* (E. characias)

BLOSSOM AND TULIPS

White parrot tulips, tinged with lime green, are one of the freshest and most textural of spring flowers. Massed together in a vase, their lettuce-like petals need no accompaniment whatsoever.

However old we are, the sight of hyacinths uncurling from tight bud or cherry trees wafting their sugar pink blossoms across the sky still fills us with irrepressible, childlike excitement. With one foot in winter and the other in summer, spring is our most unpredictable season. Warm spring breezes lull us into a sense of false optimism one day while unforgiving icy gusts hurl us back into deepest winter the next. Yet our awareness of all that urgent activity of green shoots and tiny buds around us somehow pulls us through what is often the coldest and wettest part of the year.

Blossom is readily available in the early spring months, and it comes in sprays of pale white, soft pink and deepest rose, depending on the type of fruit tree it comes from. By arranging cut stems of blossom in the house, you can fully appreciate their sculptural quality and admire the tiny florets as they continue to sprout. Here I have used a tall, elegant container, to hold a few large stems of apple and pear blossom. A scattering of blossom petals around the base also helps the arrangement blend in with its surroundings.

In fact, simplicity should be your watchword for spring — cluster primulas together in a large pot, put hyacinth bulbs in a glass tank or arrange daffodils with the first dangling branches of catkins. It is a very good season to learn how to put flowers together, because you really only need to concentrate on one or two varieties at a time to achieve a very pretty display.

Tulips are one of the most perfect of all flowers, with their elegant shapes, clean lines and sumptuous colours. In the spring, the market stalls heave with deep purples, palest yellows, stripy red and yellows, raspberry ripples, apricots and purest whites. Double tulips, parrot tulips and all the other specialist varieties are there to be snapped up at this time of the year. Even in their dying stages, tulips possess an uncanny beauty as each petal peels back and finally drifts to the foot of the vase. The illustrations on pages 32 and 33 were taken over a period of seven days and show each graceful stage of opening, burgeoning, blooming, drooping and dying.

A VALENTINE POSY

What could be more romantic than a handmade Valentine posy that comes in its own special box? I decided not to use red roses, but opted instead for this very pretty, pale colour scheme. Cream roses, tinged with pale yellow, gardenia, white lilac, guelder rose with delicate pale green bracts, ranunculus and variegated ivy are all wound into a small posy, bound with rough string, finished with a length of slippery satin ribbon and presented in a heart-shaped silver box.

Before you start grouping the flowers and foliage in one hand, you must decide how large you want your finished posy. The distance between your binding point and the flower heads will be roughly half of the finished diameter of the posy. For a posy measuring 25 cm (10 in) across, you would need to bind your material in at about 12 cm (5 in) down the stems.

METHOD

1 Strip the lower leaves off the stems of your chosen flowers, keeping just a few at the top of the sprays. You now need to group the stems in one hand, starting with your central stem. Add stems one at a time from the right and spiral the posy slightly after each addition. Keep all the stems slightly angled but meeting at the same binding point.

2 Keep checking your posy from above to make sure you are satisfied with the position of the flowers and foliage. Add small buds and large leaves last so that they frame your central blooms. When you have attached all your material, wind twine round your binding point to secure it. Finish off with a length of satin ribbon in an appropriate colour.

TRANSPARENT TANKS

MINIATURE DAFFODILS

Miniature daffodils are best observed close up, so that you can fully appreciate their delicate perfection. Here I have potted them in a textural landscape with light sand, dark sphagnum moss, pale lichen and broken terracotta – rather as though you have stumbled on a forgotten corner of the potting shed. A small pot of ivy bursting through to the surface links the plant world with the purely textural world below. Again, I have positioned the roots against a darker surface so that they can be seen clearly.

BLOSSOM

Glass is a very attractive material for arrangements of flowers, foliage and bare branches, not only because it allows light to pass through it, but its transparent qualities show you what is going on below the water as well as above. You can create fascinating effects with plant roots, stems and bulbs and use your means of supporting them – pebbles, marbles, twigs and gravel – as an integral part of the display. In this arrangement I have balanced about 10 stems of blossom in the tank and held them aloft with a simple grid of sticks.

NARCISSI TREE

Scented narcissi fill the room with a delectable fragrance and brilliant layers of orange and buttermilk petals. Here I have bunched together about thirty stems to maximize on their colours and create a sort of topiary tree. In this instance, I have filled the tank to create a verdant spring bank, a stylized interpretation of what you might find in the country. The tank is first filled with pre-soaked foam, and then the stems are added, packed tightly in to form a sculptured tree. The sides and top are packed with sphagnum moss.

HYACINTHS

Here is a tribute to our childlike fascination with hyacinth bulbs, giving a window on the stringy roots below as well as the fleshy, scented flowers above. Before planting up the tank with six potted hyacinths, I added a layer of grey beach pebbles. These not only look very effective, but they also offer a layer of support to the bulbs without hiding all their roots. I then covered the smooth, grey pebbles with water and sat the bulbs on top, so that the roots could reach down to the water reservoir below.

CATKINS AND DAFFODILS

Catkins and daffodils complement each other very effectively – the sparse and restrained textures of the former contrasting with the voluptuous, fleshy qualities of the latter. Here I have deliberately tried to emphasize this contrast and reproduce their natural environment by suspending most of the catkins above the daffodils rather than mixing them up at the same level.

METHOD

1 For this arrangement you will need a fairly wide-necked vase which will hold a quantity of broad-leaved foliage. Starting on the left-hand side of the arrangement, insert a piece of variegated ivy so that it extends right down to the bottom of the vase. Fill in around the long fronds of ivy with berried ivy leaves, placing the broad leaves around the mouth of the vase.

3 Add more foliage to the right side of the vase, allowing it to extend slightly below the rim. Try to keep the arrangement deliberately asymmetrical so that it looks elegant and natural. Insert the daffodils – both flowers and buds – among the foliage, spacing them fairly evenly. I have used two colours – pale cream and a sunshine yellow – which complement each other nicely.

2 Insert several stems of catkins in the centre of the vase, keeping them tall so that the catkins are visible above the central foliage.

4 Finally, add a small spray of catkins lower down but towards the front – this links the main stems of catkins to the rest of the arrangement.

A VASE OF TULIPS

SPRING PEDESTAL

There may be times when you are called on to make a really large arrangement, perhaps for a wedding or an anniversary party. Here I have gone to town with a 12-foot-high spring pedestal arrangement, complete with branches of magnolia, lilac and pussy willow. The size may seem intimidating, but the principles are much the same as for any arrangement, except that you have to make sure your foundations are completely firm and your vase is large and heavy enough to support the weight of the branches. Make sure you create a sense of movement by allowing tall stems to reach out at the sides and the top, and allow some branches to trail down to the floor. Try to cluster stems of one kind together, adding more of the same at staggered intervals, instead of positioning things exactly opposite each other. Allow your fullest blooms to sit low and centrally.

3 Add guelder rose at the extremities of the arrangement. Insert more magnolia and pussy willow in clusters and at different positons throughout. Avoid making your arrangement symmetrical. Towards the centre of the arrangement, add large-headed flowers – camellias, Queen of the Night tulips, Primula obconica and gardenias. Keep the gardenias in their pots and stake through their drainage holes so that they can extend out on dowel stalks. Add flowers from side to side, but not symmetrically.

METHOD

1 First line your chosen container with polythene, and then fill it with pre-soaked blocks of florist's foam, building them up over the height of the container. Here I used about six blocks as my urn was quite deep. For extra support, cover the foam with tape and chicken wire - this will stop heavy branches ripping through the foam.

2 Determine the height by inserting a stem of pussy willow in the centre back of the vase. Insert more long stems at the sides of the arrangement, such as branches of magnolia and fragrant lilac. To soften and extend the base, push the jasmine up into the foam overlapping the rim, so that it hangs down at a natural angle.

4 Tulips are inserted lower down as they have shorter stems and always look far more effective if they are allowed to droop. Their deep hue also looks good centrally. Finally, fill the back in with foliage, keeping the whole arrangement full and rounded rather than flat. This not only looks more professional, but it helps to stabilize it.

MOTHER'S DAY TRUG

Mother's Day becomes more commercial every year, and we are bombarded with present ideas on every front. Flowers, however, will always play a significant role in a Mothering Sunday, and if you can make a personal selection of your mother's favourite flowers, the gift will be especially treasured. If you have the confidence and the time, why not make her a posy – the technique is explained on page 26 – or a long lasting arrangement, such as the one shown here.

A forget-me-knot blue Somerset trug filled with deep purple and buttermilk yellow primulas, grape hyacinths and variegated ivy makes a very handsome Mother's Day present. It is best to think of this display as a garden in miniature. The bulbs and small plants are potted directly into the polythene-lined trug and then covered with a 'lawn' of ornamental pebbles, bun moss and Spanish moss. Taller plants sit at the back, and smaller ones at the front, whilst trailing ivy spills over the edge. With careful watering, the whole assembly should last a few weeks.

Once the flowers are over, the trug can then be refilled with summer bedding plants or a selection of useful kitchen herbs, such as thyme, basil and parsley. When summer is on the wane, your trug can then be potted up with small cyclamens or filled with dried flowers.

If a trug sounds a little pricey, you could also have a go at customizing a plain wooden seedbox or a wide terracotta pot. Paint your container with some pastel or bright emulsion and then fill it with a complementary range of bulbs. Remember to choose fairly small, delicate bulbs, such as miniature irises, crocuses or tiny daffodils, and don't be tempted to overfill it.

METHOD

1 Start off by lining your trug or other container with a piece of stout polythene to make it waterproof. Fill it with some broken pieces of pot for drainage and cover these with a layer of compost.

2 Take your chosen plants out of their containers and pot up the taller ones first. If you are using a trug, just remember to leave enough room around the handle so it can be carried easily.

3 Water the arrangement and then fill in any gaps between the plants with bun moss, and perhaps a few pretty pebbles. Tease out the Spanish moss and let it tumble down the sides of the trug.

EASTER EXTRAVAGANZA

Easter weekend really calls for a special arrangement of flowers, and I like to choose something unusual for the festive celebrations. Instead of the typical white-yellow colour scheme so readily associated with Easter, I have opted for pretty sugar colours interlaced with rich foliage. The peach, apricot and pink crinkled layers of the parrot tulips and the ranunculus reminds me of the folds of Fortuny silk – rich, heavy and exotic – nestling around the delicate heads of Icelandic poppies. As the flowers themselves are so beautiful, I have kept the actual arrangement very simple. A colourful medium-sized jug adds an air of informality to the display and allows the flowers to hang heavily over the rim. I arranged the parrot tulips first, and then filled in towards the centre with the ranunculus and the frailer poppies, interweaving the bright green foliage of euphorbia and the red-leafed eucalyptus and mahonia with the flowers. Height is built up gradually, until the layers of flowers support each other's weight. Finally, a few painted Easter eggs are strewn around the base to emphasize the seasonal connection, although these normally disappear fairly quickly!

SUMMER

SUMMER FLOWERS

In northern Europe, summer seems a very fleeting experience. If spring is late and autumn early, summer may be confined to about a month in terms of really good weather. This is probably why we tend to seize every opportunity that the season offers – rushing off for picnics as soon as the sun peeps out, gulping down strawberries and cream and charging down to the beach for a freezing dip in the sea. Oh, how we envy those southern Mediterraneans who can look nonchalantly at a brilliant blue sea and sip sangria on their terraces for at least half of the year!

Yet whether the sun is shining or not, the garden still offers treasures for the flower arranger which will only be available from a florist at other times of the year. Colours range from sharp citruses, fuchsia pinks, vibrant reds and explosive yellows to pale creams, silvers and aqua-tinted blues. Not only are the colours more varied but the scents are headier and the blossoms more voluptuous now.

When choosing flowers for a summer arrangement, try to look beyond the predictable blooms that are available throughout the year. Just as you make full use of your every free sunny day, always make the most of the flowers that are short-lived and sun-loving. The ones

that really have the smell and zing of summer – tea roses, peonies, scabious, cornflowers and sweet peas, to name a few. Hydrangeas are incredibly versatile for most arranging, and also one of the best flowers for drying, so they are well worth growing if you can. Then there are all the wonderful old-fashioned flowers such as stocks, verbena, busy lizzies, rudbeckia, poppies and honesty that ramble in the cottage garden or beneath the window. Use this profusion of summer blooms while you can, because just as you have become accustomed to their presence, they are already beginning to pale and droop.

1 hydrangeas 2 stocks 3 pinks 4 peonies 5 ranunculus 6 foxgloves 7 delphiniums

SUMMER FOLIAGE

I always think that the first two months of summer are the most intoxicating time of the year, although they quickly give way to a rather scorched and tired looking landscape after July. Yet in May and June the countryside is verdant and aromatic, and town and country gardens burgeon with floral activity of every kind. This is the season when the division between foliage and flower becomes faintly absurd, as hardy shrubs errupt into starry white flowers, and trees bend down with candy pink and waxy florescences.

Summer is particulary good for grey foliage, with cotton lavender (santolina), eucalyptus, sage, rue, and *Stachys lanata* (lamb's ears) to choose from. Grey looks wonderful with any colour, but particularly white, as Vita Sackville-West understood, when she planned her white garden at Sissinghurst, interweaving rue, lavender and helichrysums with ivory tree-peonies and scented roses. Even the smallest garden will yield an amazing palette of foliage if carefully planted – from light feathery limes to glossy dark greens. I use hostas a great deal in arrangements, as they add weight and support to slender stems, and there are a legion varieties to choose from. Eucalyptus is always versatile, and long-lasting, and I recently matched it up with vivid

long-stemmed orange marigolds to great effect.
Ceanothus, spiraea (also called bride's blossom) and
guelder rose are other favourites that last well in water,
whilst frondy foliages such as fennel, alchemilla and cow
parsley will lighten heavier summer flowers.

And finally a plea to remember all the climbing foliages –
honeysuckle, jasmine, nasturtium, clematis and Virginia
creeper, which can be so effective for extending a large
floral display, such as the pedestal arrangement on page
35. As long as you build up your floral foam above the
level of the container, you can insert these trailing stems
at an upward angle so that they hang down gracefully .

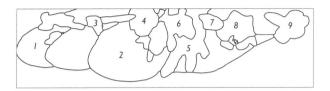

1 grey hosta *2 variegated hosta* *3 spiraea* *4 guelder rose*
(Viburnum betulifolium) *5 fig* *6 euphorbia* *7 ceanothus*
8 Valerian opulus *9 clematis*

MAKING A BOUQUET

Bouquets are lovely gifts to give to a loved one, friend, or colleague to say thank you or congratulations. Here I have created three colour-themed bouquets using fairly common summer flowers. The pink bouquet (left) is a combination of miniature tea roses, with larkspur and sedum adding texture and contrast. With all the posies I have steered away from making them symmetrical, to capture that haphazard beauty of the summer garden. Shades of soft creamy white make a beautiful posy – marguerites, roses and hydrangeas form the body of the posy, whilst fronds of honeysuckle extend the shape and add perfume. Finally, a small colourful posy of purple and grey makes an interesting variation. Purple asters, cotton lavender and lisianthus all combine well and are offset by cineraria.

For any posy, you need to spiral the flowers and foliage in your hand, starting with the middle of the posy. Insert your stems at a slight angle and bind them together at the same point down the stem.

CONDITIONING ROSES

When you buy roses from a florist or a market stall, you may occasionally be disappointed to find the blooms drooping when you unwrap them. Yet most of the time, this effect is reversible. Once you have trimmed off any thorns and cut off the ends of the stems, prepare a bowl of boiling water. Plunge the ends of the stems in the water, taking care to shield the blooms from the steam – you should wrap the flowers in newspaper, keeping the wilted flowers upright. Take the stems out after two minutes and put them in cold water. This should remove any airlocks and allow water to be taken up. Despite all these precautions, you may yet find that your flowers do not last very long. This may be because they have been poorly treated after harvesting. Sometimes flowers that are grown intensively for one occasion are in poor condition before they even reach the florist – Valentine roses often seem pre-programmed to keel over on 15 February, for instance. The only preventative action you can take is to find a reliable supplier.

METHOD

1 First remove any leaves that are likely to appear below the water in the vase, as they will quickly turn the water cloudy.

3 Cut off the ends of the stems on a diagonal to allow maximum exposure to the boiling water.

2 Trim rose thorns with a sharp knife. Make sure you trim with the blade moving away from you.

4 Plunge the cut stems into the water, carefully protecting the rose heads from the steam as you do so.

LONG-STEMMED ROSES

One of the most effective vessels for displaying roses is a tall glass vase. Fill the vase to at least three-quarters full with water, as the stems take up water along their length.

A ROSE TREE

Nicole roses look spectacular when bound together in a tight posy and displayed as a topiary tree. Bind the roses below the heads and again lower down with green twine. Then place the ends in pre-soaked florist's foam. Cover the top with a layer of carpet moss.

ARRANGING ROSES

Nicole roses are one of the loveliest varieties of early summer rose, with their sumptuous velvety petals, showing red on the inner side but a pale creamy white on the reverse. Here I have put together five very different arrangements to show you how versatile just a single bunch of flowers can be.

A JUG OF ROSES
For a more informal look, try putting red roses with blues, limes and pinks. Here I have used my roses at a slightly lower height, and added blue ceanothus, cowslips, London pride, wallflowers, euphorbia and Photinia 'Red Robin'.

ROSE AND LAVENDER POT-POURRI
It is sometimes very hard to throw away a special bunch of roses. If you do decide to dry them, hang them upside down in a warm, airy place. Here I simply used some dried lavender and grey cineraria leaves as a bed for my dried rose heads. You can also revive the scent with pot-pourri oil.

ROSE BOWL
Roses are stunning as these look spectacular cut down very short and placed in a rose bowl, allowing you to look down on their velvet petals and drink in their full beauty.

SWEET PEAS

Sweet peas are the butterflies of summer flowers with their amazingly delicate petals poised on hairy grey stalks. Narrow-necked and wide-based vases are most suitable for holding together these very slender stems, allowing the blooms to tumble out in a profusion of colour. Notice how none of them is quite the same shade – apricot melts into soft pink, which bursts into brick red before fading back to white. A wonderful kaleidoscope of gauzy colour.

SUMMER NIGHTS

An arrangement of ripe fruits and fragrant herbs, interspersed with creamy scented candles, makes a stunning dinner party display and is particularly lovely on a hot summer evening. Using a tier of misted glass saucers balanced on tall metal stands, I was able to create a feeling of overflowing profusion by layering and cascading the plant material and fruits (a similar effect could be achieved with an elegant cakestand or a large candlestick).

METHOD

1 Secure the large candles on the top two layers of the cakestand to start with, by fixing them in place with plasticine. If you can get hold of them, use scented candles instead of ordinary ones.

2 Then add some pieces of fruit to each of the three layers. I opted for a colour scheme of greens and reds and selected choice items that my guests would enjoy as a finale to their meal – grapes, plums, greengages, figs and pears – putting the heaviest ones on the bottom tier.

3 Fill in around the fruit with small sprigs of green and grey foliage, such as sage, rosemary, parsley and rue. It also looks very pretty if you add a few clusters of sedum. The attractive succulent leaves have a pinkish hue and add extra texture and colour to the overall arrangement.

4 In the bottom layer, fill some small containers with water and float scented night lights in them. Finally spray the whole arrangement to finish.

Wrapping candles in vine leaves is simple and highly effective. First wrap a piece of double-sided tape around the middle of the candle. Place the candle on a young vine leaf and draw the edges up around the candle, pressing them together against the sticky tape. As a finishing touch, tie the candles with green garden string, inserting a sprig of rosemary beneath the top knot. The candle can be used on its own or in an arrangement but never let the flame burn down near the flowers or leaves.

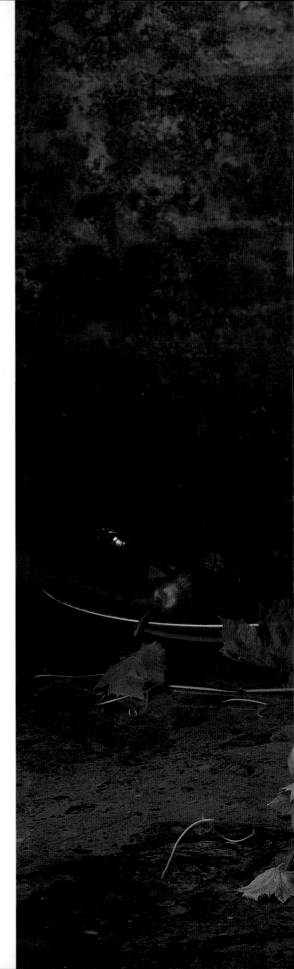

A COTTAGE GARDEN

At the height of summer, I take great pleasure in making up a really vibrant, abundant arrangement which seems to topple over the sides of the container. Here I have used a profusion of bright, scented blooms, including foxgloves, scented stocks, lilacs, Solomon's seal, guelder roses, hydrangeas, ranunculus, delphiniums, coppery leaves and rhododendrons. With pinks, corals, purples, creams and blues all vying for attention, this luscious mixture of flowers recalls those burgeoning summer gardens, which miraculously display a multitude of different flowers in the smallest of spaces.

METHOD

1 Start by building up a grid of adhesive tape over a fairly wide and deep container. The tape is a cunning way to hold the flowers loosely in place. Then insert flowers that have a natural propensity for leaning – the lilac, guelder roses, stocks and foxgloves.

3 Add a splash of rich colour with a spray of rhododendrons and complementary coppery leaves. These 'hot' colours go surprisingly well with blues and pinks if they are used in a bold way, and if your arrangement is as eclectic and exuberant as this one

2 Build up the back of the container with the tallest stems, such as foxgloves and delphiniums, and then move towards the centre with the large-headed blooms, such as the peonies.

4 Insert smaller stems last, using them to fill in any gaps. The ranunculus adds bright splashes of colour, whilst the stocks will scent the air with their delicious perfume.

PINKS AND WHITES

Pyramidal blooms of *Hydrangea paniculata* make an effervescent display for mid-summer. Pink roses and young antirrhinums (snapdragons) add a touch of warmth and pick up the hues of the rounder variety of *Hydrangea macrophylla* (the common garden hydrangea). Once I was satisfied with the grouping of flowers, I introduced the dark tendrils of ivy to extend the arrangement downwards and provide an essential delicacy and interest throughout. It is always a good idea to balance very full and heavy heads with stems of ivy or other trailing foliage. If you pick the hydrangeas when the bracts are just beginning to open, the display will last at least a week.

Summer pinks are long-lasting and delicately perfumed. Sedum peeps out from between the pinks and ivy elongates the parameters. The arrangement is kept low and long, by using short stems at the centre and long stems to arch over the sides. With their coral red centres, the pinks pick out the deep hues of the sedum effectively.

TRUE BLUE

A study in vivid blue – with three types of flower displaying their own distinctive interpretation on the colour. Scabious are a pale velvety-blue, delicate and crumpled like pieces of scalloped tissue paper. Cornflowers are unabashedly intense – deep pools of cerulean surrounded by thickets of bristles. And finally, we have thistles, with their pineapples of aggressive prickles, bursting into plumes of softest indigo.

Whichever you prefer, try keeping each variety separate, so that their colours are undiluted perfection.

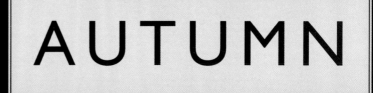

AUTUMN

AUTUMN FLOWERS

A patchwork of colours, mellowing light and periodic bursts of luxurious sunshine. Swirling mists and early frosts are portents of winter, and exuberant gusts of wind shake off the colourful leaves clinging precariously to the trees in the park. Autumn is a time I cherish for its vibrancy, moodiness and astonishing beauty. As for flowers, the change of colours from season to season is surely more dramatic between summer and autumn than at any other time of year. The soft lilacs, brilliant whites, fuchsias and citrons of those long, light days seem to slip away with the first cool winds, to be replaced by the rich, earthy colours of autumn – deep reds, golds, bronzes and russets. Some of the more delectable summer flowers that have been dried can be brought out now. Peonies, roses and nigella have a frail and delicate beauty when dried, allowing them to retain something of their summer zenith. Hydrangeas and ammobium are even more beautiful when their colours are softened and their textures toughened by air drying.

PREVIOUS PAGE
A dramatic and textural blend of deep crimsons and purples, featuring ornamental cabbage, love-lies-bleeding, heather, blackberries, Virginia creeper and pansies.

Yet in resorting to dried flowers you may be neglecting an array of Renaissance colours and bitter-sweet fragrances. Feverfew, golden rod, asters and zinnias are some of the delights in early autumn; fleshy sedum, bronze chrysanthemums and deep crimson heather then provide glowing colour in the darker months towards winter. During these months of harvest and gleaning, go for flowers that suggest the home-grown, that blend with the polished-wood colours of foliage, or that evoke those splendidly romantic feelings of nostalgia and mortality that Keats and Shelley expressed so poignantly in their poetry.

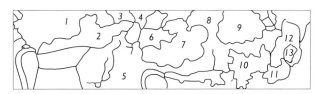

1 Trachelium caeruleum *2* erica *3* Ageratum houstonianum *4* celosia *5* Russian vine *6* September flower (Aster 'Monte Cassino') *7* dahlia *8* wall flower *9* chrysanthemum bloom and spray *10* hebe *11* anemone *12* Geraldton waxflower (Chamelaucium uncinatum) *13* lisianthus (Eustoma grandiflorum)

AUTUMN FOLIAGE AND FRUIT

On some days when the sun is as bright as a May morning, nothing can beat the sights, colours and smells of autumn – the early morning mist over the lawn, a Virginia creeper turning from leaf green to flame red against a stone wall and the earthy aroma of bonfires smouldering in the park. Leaves are symbolic of autumn, or Fall, as it is so appropriately called by our New World cousins. The kaleidoscopic colours of foliage constitute nature's final striptease before we are confronted by the nudity of winter. Often neglected, leaves make wonderful arrangements on their own, with their eclectic shades or reds, ochres, greens and browns jostling for our attention. I often gather up a selection of leaves from the garden – oak, chestnut, beech and maple – and then simply mound them up in a basket. In arrangements themselves, I tend to use the bronze branches of beech and cotinus, blushing and fleshy bergenia, and white-flecked sprays of viburnum. Ivy and holly are also abundant, and skimmias and mahonias are useful ballast as flowers become scarce.

The autumn shops are also full of knobbly gourds, striped squashes and monstrous pumpkins – the last quirky symbols of summer's fertility and the harbingers of harvest celebrations. Look out too for those

almond-coloured, satin-smooth butternut squashes, which are one of the most beautiful autumn vegetables. From the garden you can also glean other rich treasures, such as rowan berries, rose-hips, crab apples, cotoneaster, blackberries, hawthorn, pyracantha and skimmia. If you don't have access to a garden, look for windfalls in the roads and parks – apples, beechnuts, conkers and acorns – and pile them up in a wooden bowl or a favourite basket. In these simple and inexpensive ways, you can fill your home with glorious fruits and sumptuous foliage, making use of this profusion while it lasts.

I Viburnum tinus *2 cotoneaster 3 bergenia 4 hebe 5 rose-hips 6 Cornus alba 7 rose-hips 8 cotinus*

IMMORTAL POSIES

As the frost begins to nip the delicate stems of summer flowers, it is obviously quite appealing to dry some of the more suitable varieties to sustain you through the bleaker days ahead. Most flowers actually dry if they are hung up in a warm place, although of course some retain their colours and shapes much better than others. Hydrangeas are always a great success, as are nigella, lavender, yarrow and xeranthemums (or *immortelles,* as they are more poetically known). It is important to pick your flowers before they have opened completely and on a dry day. Store them in small bunches and, having bound them with string, hang them upside down in a well-ventilated warm room or an airing cupboard.

Here I decided to make some small posies from a mixture of late summer flowers and the first seasonal berries, leaving them to dry just as they are. The posies are not as perfect as those that are specially created from dried flowers, as some of the material distorts as it shrinks, but when a posy has sentimental value, or if it is just too lovely to throw away, what could be nicer than to preserve it entirely as it is ?

The pink posy contains scented geranium leaves, hydrangeas, roses, blackberries, euonymus and sedum. When dry, the roses and hydrangeas retain their colours best, but the withered blackberries and the orange seed capsules of euonymus can still be seen clearly and retain the textural interest. The yellow posy is a mixture of hydrangeas, variegated ivy *(Hedera canariensis),* solidago, marigolds, mimosa, yellow roses and matricaria. Again, the hydrangeas retain their colour well, as do the roses, and the matricaria *(Chrysanthemum parthenium)* is still clear and interesting. The bluey-green posy blends asters, hydrangeas, mint, rosemary, rue, sage, and pansies, and retains its fragrance and pale hue as it dries.

The three posies, after two weeks of air drying, are softer in hue yet still pretty mementoes to treasure.

HIPS AND HAWS

Here I have combined the last blooms of summer with the first berries and rose-hips of autumn to create an arrangement of voluptuous ripeness. Building up from the outside edge with lighter branches which drape over the edge, I then moved into the centre with taller stems and fuller flowers. More delicate blooms look better on the outer edge where they help to keep the outline of the design soft and rounded. *Hydrangea macrophylla*, with its pale green flowers tinged with terracotta, is used to fill out this grey bucket, while late marigolds and solidago add small pools of light among the reds and greens. A touch of purple is introduced with some late monkshood, while blackberries, sedum, rose-hips, hawthorn and variegated ivy *(Hedera colchica)* all point to the darker, textural materials of autumn that are now at your disposal. The most wonderful thing about this arrangement is that it will dry slowly and gracefully, and can then be admired throughout the winter months. Simply take the arrangement out of water. Bind the stems tightly with twine or string and hang the whole bunch upside-down to dry for about two months.

In this arrangement I have put together a collection of late summer and early autumn flora to capture that brief period when the seasons overlap. These delicate, gentle flowers, without a dominant centre, suggest a sort of hedgerow grouping. Buddleja, golden rod, feverfew, bracken, privet, fennel, blackberries, elderberries, white campion, rose-hips, and guelder rose berries (Viburnum opulus) *are all included, and a glazed earthenware container blends in with their soft tones.*

ANEMONE TREES

Anemones are some of the brightest flowers of the autumn. Their velvety, Byzantine blooms look wonderful clustered tightly together. Although most people choose to put them in a small low vase rather than actually 'arrange' them, the long-stemmed varieties give you much more scope for creativity. Here I have used a generous bundle of long-stemmed anemones to make a container tree. This arrangement will last for up to a week and just needs topping up with some fresh water each day to keep it blooming.

METHOD

1 First choose a small bucket or low container which will easily hold a small glass. The anemone stems will be inserted into this glass, so check that it is wide enough to hold them securely. The outer container should ideally be about a third of the height of your flowers and, obviously, opaque.

3 When you have a full and rounded posy, tie the anemones tightly with twine below the flowers and again further down your stems to secure. Then trim the ends of the stems so that they will sit evenly on the bottom of the glass. Don't cut too much off, however, as the stems need to be quite tall.

2 Form your tree with about twenty anemones. Holding the first stem, start from the middle of the bunch by placing each stem parallel to the next. The stems should be kept very neat and straight.

4 Put the anemones in the glass container, and then place it in your bucket or vase. Finally, cover the top of the bucket with a layer of soft green carpet moss so that the glass is completely concealed.

ZINNIAS

Like dahlias, zinnias are exuberant and hardy flowers that come in intense colour ranges. Here they need no other accompaniment than a brightly coloured vase. I have deliberately kept the arrangement full and compact.

DAHLIAS

On days when autumn rain sheets down on lead-coloured pavements, I suggest you go for colour for all it's worth – a huge jug of purple anemones, a cloud of golden asters or a vase of dolly-mixture dahlias.

AUTUMN WEDDING

A baroque posy and headdress of pale pink, yellow and fuchsia-coloured roses, with rose-hips, love-lies-bleeding, blackberries, hydrangeas, eucalyptus, heather and sedum. I always think weddings that use flowers in season are much nicer than those that rely on imported flowers. This wreath will add warmth to an ivory dress with splashes of rich colour – just ensure the blackberries are not too ripe or your splashes will be permanent! Although I would suggest that you leave the florist to make the headdress, as this requires wiring, an informal posy such as this can be made at home and is simply bound with twine. I find its random quality very appealing, suggestive of the old-fashioned tussie-mussies of herbs and cottage flowers favoured by the Victorians. Choose flowers that will last all day out of water – roses, chrysanthemums, September flowers (*Aster* 'Monte Cassino') and hydrangeas are all contenders. Berries and ivy are also attractive and long-lasting, and help to highlight the flowers. When deciding where to position flowers and foliage, group the flowers in your hand and try them in various arrangements. Colours can be used to emphasize shape, and foliage to add softness and contrast. Large-headed flowers are best placed towards the centre of the posy to draw the eye in, and smaller heads or daintier buds are best around the edge where they help to soften the outlines.

This pretty basket is filled with rose petals so that guests can throw natural confetti over the bride and groom when they emerge from the church. Two small pieces of pre-soaked florist's foam are carefully wired to the inside of the basket so that they are hidden from view. Small open roses, skimmia berries, rosemary and white heather are then inserted into the foam. The floral decoration is discreet enough to allow guests easy access to the petals within. Finally, fronds of ivy and red eucalyptus trail down the sides and wind round the handle.

METHOD *(for the posy)*

1 Start with your central stem, holding it between your thumb and forefinger. Attach a length of twine about halfway down the stem. If you want your final posy diameter to be 25 cm (10 in), make your binding point half this distance - i.e. 12.5 cm (5 in) down the stems.

2 Lay your second stem at a slight angle to the first stem, but attach it with the twine at the same binding point. It may help to add flowers from the right, turning the posy slightly in an anti-clockwise direction after each

flower. If you find this difficult, just position the flowers at the same binding point but at different angles, and keep checking the arrangement from above as you go.

3 When you have added all the material, bind the base of the stems with the twine several times to make sure it is secure. Finish with a ribbon to hide the twine.

4 Keep the posy in a cool place and mist with water before setting forth.

CHRYSANTHEMUMS

Chrysanthemums, for me, are the flowers of autumn, often seen for sale in jam jars down winding country lanes or displayed in glorious profusion in local harvest shows and flower competitions. Although they have often been dismissed in recent years as vulgar and garish, they now seem to be enjoying a huge revival as everyone turns away from city chic and back to country simplicity. I particularly love the large-headed varieties, and the bronze hues are wonderful with blushing Virginia creeper and unadorned terracotta. The flowers should last a full week or more, and their distinctive herby aroma will drift gently through the house.

A SILVER BIRCH LOG BASKET

A silver birch log basket makes a stunning fireplace decoration, and is fairly simple to make. I planted my basket up with bright heather, as its woody quality matches the silver birch very well, but you could choose any number of long-lasting plants, such as azalea, solanum or cyclamen. Put the pots directly into the basket, or line the whole basket with polythene before filling it with compost. Remember to water the plants regularly and remove any dead or wilting flowers so that your fireplace centrepiece is always in pristine condition for guests or family to admire.

METHOD

1 First saw lengths of logs to form the sides and bottom of the basket, using a hand saw. I have used four 45-cm (18-in) pieces for the lengths, four 45-cm pieces for the bottom and six 25-cm (10-in) pieces for the widths. You will also need some raffia, rope or twine to tie the logs firmly together.

3 For the sides, place the logs on top of one another, and as you work tie the pieces together with several knots in order to secure well.

4 Once the basket is constructed, squeeze moss into all the gaps between the logs, pushing it in firmly .

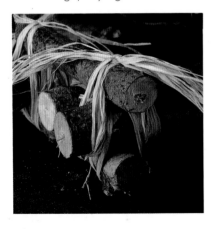

2 For the bottom of the basket, lay your four logs parallel like a raft, then use lengths of raffia, rope or twine to bind the logs firmly together at the ends so that they do not move.

5 Finally, either line the basket with strong polythene before filling with compost and plants, or insert pots directly into the basket. I also fill my baskets with heaps of leaves.

APPLE WREATH

Apples are abundant at this time of the year. If you are lucky enough to have a tree in your garden, this wreath will be particularly apt. For special occasions such as harvest or Hallowe'en, an apple wreath is very welcoming and cheering for guests. This wreath is given substance with hunks of tree bark, hydrangeas, moss and ivy, which all reflect the colours of the ripe apples and suggest the pot-pourri of the orchard floor. Instead of applying the material in layers, it is better to work clockwise in quarters, so that you complete each section in turn before moving on to the next one.

METHOD

1 For this simple apple wreath, you need to buy a wire wreath frame from your florist. Then fill your frame with some pre-soaked sphagnum moss, binding it in place with florist's twine. The moss needs to be fairly compact in order to hold the heavier materials later. See the ivy wreath on page 97 for further details of binding the moss into the wreath.

2 Working on your first quarter of the wreath, pin a layer of bun moss or lichen on top of the wire frame filled with sphagnum. Secure this top layer of moss with small pieces of medium-gauge florist's wire, bent into little hairpins.

3 Next add some pieces of bark and ivy. Push more hairpins of wire through the bark and over the ivy stems so that the ends of wire appear at the back of the wreath. Bend the exposed ends back into the wreath from behind. Cover the bark with a little more moss to blend it in naturally.

4 Next apply an apple by taking a piece of wire about 25 cm (10 in) long and pushing it through the middle of the apple (at right angles to the stalk). Make sure the wire protrudes from both sides equally, and then pull down the ends to form a hairpin. Twist the wire together at the base of the apple a couple of times, and then insert the wire and apple into the moss. Again allow the wires to penetrate the frame, and bend back the ends into the frame. The apple must nestle in the moss, not stand proud of it, so pin on some more moss to blend in the edges.

5 Add hydrangea heads, pinning them on in the same way, and more moss. Then proceed clockwise to the next quarter of the wreath, and repeat the process until your wreath is covered.

Note: the wreath will keep for at least two weeks on an outside door and you can replace any withered apples.

A table arrangement of vegetables is always impressive for a church display, a harvest supper or just a sumptuous kitchen decoration. Here I have created a display of abundance, a rich tapestry of colours to record the harvest of the year. The home-grown vegetables are fixed onto a mound of florist's foam with strong raffia-covered wire or staked with small pieces of cane. Most roots and leaves are deliberately left intact. The marvellous lime-green brassica is called Roman or Romanesco cauliflower, and, with its stunning sculpted, spiral swirls, it makes the perfect focus for the arrangement. Do look out for it in the autumn as it is a true visual delight.

SMALL TREES

RED PEPPER TREE

This wonderfully coiffured tablepiece is made by weaving red chilli peppers over and through each other until you have a rounded, compact thatch. These peppers may still be a rarity in some towns, but I have noticed that they have become far more commonplace in recent years. If you can't find any, ask your local florist if she will stock them specially for you. Not only do the peppers dry successfully, but their rich colours will glow in a dark corner and add a touch of exotica to a dark autumn day. Do note, however, that chilli peppers are quite fragile and tricky to bend. You really need to set aside some time for this arrangement so that you can carefully and slowly bend them into place. You may need to try it several times before you are really satisfied with the shape.

Small topiary trees are great fun to make at this time of the year, and the principles are not difficult to master. Basically, you need to choose a fairly firm type of stem, that can be inserted into a pot of florist's foam, and then trimmed or bent into shape. You should aim to make your topiary tree a very precise and definite shape – nothing too fussy – which can be appreciated for its bold lines from a distance. Ears of wheat look very seasonal and smart and can be inserted into a pot of floral foam at different heights to resemble a wheat sheaf (see page 14). Broom and red peppers also look very chic in the following types of trees.

METHOD

Broom is a very satisfying material to work with, as it can be cropped like hair, twisted, coiled and even plaited. It will then dry and last for the whole season. You can insert a wedge of broom into a pot of floral foam and simply trim the ends, or bend the ends back in on themselves to create a neat knot of broom.

1 Fill a terracotta pot with dry florist's foam to just below the rim. Insert stems of orange and red peppers into the pot so that they are all standing upright and at approximately the same height.

2 Bend down the upper third of all the stems one by one and push them carefully towards the middle, weaving the stems into each other. Take care not to snap any of the fragile stems.

3 Gradually, tuck the ends into the centre of the pot and tease out the doubled stems to form a rounded tree.

4 Cover the base of the peppers and any visible foam with some fine, tendrilly moss such as sphagnum. Finish off the design with a deep red upholstery cord to complement the rich colours, weaving a little sprig of peppers into the cord to decorate the front of the pot.

THANKSGIVING SWAG

Here, to decorate a Thanksgiving feast, I have made a swag recalling the simple and wholesome life of the early settlers in America. The swag is very easy, as the foundation is a string of twisted dried hops, which you can buy from florists and markets in the early weeks of autumn.

METHOD

1 First check that your string of hops is long enough to reach along your table. Obviously, the more times you catch it up, the longer it needs to be in order to swag effectively. Then place your chosen cloth over the table (it helps if it is a fairly coarse one which you don't mind pinning things to – hessian is ideal).

3 Before you attach the hop swag to the cloth, decorate the length of it with small clusters of red and blue dried hydrangeas. Attach the string of hops to the table corners by tying the string firmly around the two free ends. Leave enough string to tie on the rope at the last stage.

2 Pin one 25-cm (10-in) piece of string to each end of the table, securing it firmly with glass-headed pins, adding more of the same at any intervals along the table where you might wish to catch up the swag. Each pin needs to be at the centre of the piece of string, so that you have 12.5 cm (5 in) hanging either side.

4 Pin the swag up along the table, securing it with your strategically placed string. Alternatively, you can just leave it to droop from the two corner supports. Finally, take two lengths of old rope and tie them both to the string at the corners of the table, allowing the rope to tumble down both of the sides.

WINTER

WINTER FLOWERS

The months between December and early March are dark ones indeed. Trees stretch across a bleak grey horizon like a series of black inkblots, and the garden stands dejected and denuded, holding its breath until the dark months pass. Relief comes when the sun pierces the blanket of grey and lights up every crack of the garden with brilliant sunshine. Hoar frost or a sprinkling of snow transforms the bare branches with a host of diamond shards and cloaks the horrors lurking in the garden with a glittering mantle. In these moments of winter magic, we suddenly appreciate the sculptural quality of the vegetation in this minimalist landscape.

When it comes to winter flowers, I like to work with two main palettes – white and red. There is a variety of white hot-house flowers available, some of which have a spare, minimalist beauty; others, a delicious perfume. Some of my favourite pale and white flowers are waxy stephanotis, which is as beautiful as it is fragrant, delicate jasmine, exotic and bold amaryllis, and hardy cyclamen. The garden may also proffer snowdrops, winter-flowering rhododendrons and azaleas, flowering viburnum and Christmas roses. In fact I find all the hellebore family stunning, with their pale green bracts, and one of the most beautiful plants to arrange.

The reds are a colour range that will always prevail in the months between November and January, bringing instant warmth, luxury and abundance into the home. Deep crimson azaleas, scarlet poinsettia, blood red cyclamen, red roses and claret winter-flowering pansies are some of the florists' blooms. The garden contains very few red flowers at this time of the year, except perhaps some winter-flowering azaleas or rhododendrons, but the deficiency can easily be made up with fiery berries and fruits. Red can be teamed very successfully with blues and purples too, so do try arrangements like the one on page 114 if tired of Christmas colours.

1 arum lily **2** Euphorbia fulgens **3** *Christmas rose* **4** Eucharis grandiflora **5** *spray roses* **6** stephanotis **7** *jasmine*

WINTER FOLIAGE

Foliage is your best friend at Christmas. Bundles of natural foliage will always out-shine the gaudy fripperies of department stores. If you pick spruce, herbs or other scented greenery, you will be able to fill your room with aromatic fragrances at the same time. However, you don't need to go to the expense of adding flowers, except perhaps for the festive week itself. Remember to choose a selection of different shapes and colours so that you make the most of the seasonal variety. If you put dark green holly and laurel together they may be indistinguishable from a distance, but if you use a contrasting variegated holly, it will set the laurel off nicely.

Displays of foliage and mossy wreaths can also be punctuated with intense splashes of colour from some of the many seasonal berries, such as rowan, holly, solanum, cotoneaster, and pyracantha. Alternatively, paper ribbons, or colourful fabrics will enliven your wreaths or swags in a very economical fashion.

Don't forget to make use of all the textural and colourful branches and twigs at your disposal, such as larch, eucalyptus pods bursting with fluffy yellow seeds, willow, hazel and dogwood. In a large vase these can look superb on their own, or touched with white and gold paint to create a frosted effect, they can make very

stylish, alternative Christmas trees, which have the merit of having no pine needles to drop.

You will probably have realized by now that I am also a confirmed fan of indoor topiary. The colourful chilli pepper tree that I prepared in the autumn will now have dried, and can be used successfully as a Christmas table arrangement. There are many other ways of creating smart and long-lasting topiary trees for winter, and I have put together a selection of my favourites on the following pages. With a little practice you can soon become adept at creating all sorts of miniature trees – they make lovely presents and smart decorations.

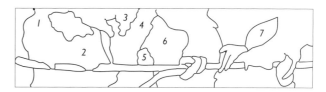

*1 eucalyptus pods **2** berried ivy **3** eucalyptus **4** larch twigs covered in lichen **5** red pepper berries **6** variegated holly **7** Garrya elliptica (tassel bush)*

WREATHS

Wreaths are perennially popular floral decorations, and never more so than at Christmas. The circle of the wreath has ancient associations with fertility, renewal and the triumph of life over death – all highly appropriate as we celebrate the solstice, the shortest day of the year, and look forward to the return of the sun. In many ancient societies wreaths were the main floral decorations at weddings, with simple wreaths of myrtle, hawthorn or verbena being presented to the bride and groom as fertility tokens.

With a little care and attention you will be able to make a wreath that looks extremely professional and effective, so it is worth mastering the basic technique. You can buy a basic wreath frame if you don't want to make one, and there are several types available, including circular and oval frames made from wire, twigs or florist's foam. A wreath made from green foam is best if you are intending to lay it down flat on a table and insert fresh flowers. This sort of frame provides a good solid structure and it can be watered each day. It is ideal for something like an Advent wreath, which is traditionally decorated with spruce, red flowers and four candles, each representing one week of Advent. Wreaths made from twigs are excellent if you are using dried materials in small quantities – the twigs are meant to be seen, so you need only a minimal amount of extra decoration, such as cinnamon sticks, walnuts, pine cones or gold ribbon.

WIRE FRAMES

A wire frame, however, is normally the best choice for a door wreath, which tends to be decorated with heavier, evergreen material. Normally, the frame is filled and covered with soft pre-soaked sphagnum moss, and then bound tightly with twine – the moss provides padding as well as a water reserve for the floral material. Any strands of moss are trimmed off with scissors before the decoration is applied. Always decorate your wreath by completing small sections, before moving clockwise to the next section.

Fixing a wreath to your door or wall is simplicity itself if you have a hook or door knob to slip it over. If not, you just need to make a ribbon loop at the top of the wreath. Put the loop on before you attach any foliage by knotting it through the wire, or round the foam. Finish off the wreath with a bow of some really beautiful fabric – such as shot silk or colourful tartan – or go for the natural look and complete with some crunchy paper ribbon. Spray your wreath from time to time to keep it fresh.

A PLAIN IVY WREATH

A sleek wreath is simple to make with only glossy ivy leaves on top of a moss foundation.

1 Fill a plain wire frame with tightly packed sphagnum moss, and bind it in place with twine.

2 Wire the outer and inner leaves first at the point where the leaf joins the stem. Then attach the centre leaf last so that it covers the wires either side. Progress clockwise until complete.

A ROPE WREATH

The rope wreath is a long lasting and extremely pretty circle of foliage. Its effect is essentially textural, with eucalyptus pods, old rope and lichen all creating layers of interest. Everything in the wreath should dry gracefully, so the effort required is more than justified by the time it takes. The complementary colours of the lichen and the bursting eucalyptus seedpods, revealing their fluffy yellow seeds, also lighten the foundation layer of ivy, and allow you to appreciate each floral component from a distance. It is important to get a sense of movement into this wreath by using longish pieces of plant material which can stretch away from the core of the wreath in a sort of spiral. I like to think that the final effect looks rather like a spinning Catherine wheel with all its energetic foliage radiating out.

METHOD

In contrast with the sleek ivy wreath, this circlet of red pepper berries and chilli peppers bristles with vitality and colour. If you can't get hold of these berries, just make sure that you use a variety of different berries – holly, cotoneaster and rose-hips, for example – to set against your dark green leaves. Notice how the material looks full and proud of the surface, with the berries in small clumps as they grow naturally. All the berries are wired on in clusters with pieces of medium-gauge wire.

1 Fill a wire wreath frame with pre-soaked sphagnum moss (see the wreath on page 97), ensuring that you achieve a constant density and thickness of moss as you go. Bind twine around the whole frame to secure the filling. Trim any loose edges of moss with scissors. You should now have a smooth, even 'canvas' to work upon.

2 Begin to wire on your material by working in small one-sixth sections, moving clockwise around the wreath. You need to pin on all your material, including your pieces of rope, with medium-gauge wire bent into a hairpin shape. The wire ends need to be pushed right through the frame and then bent back into it. It is a good idea to pin your large ivy leaves on first of all as they act as a foundation layer of green for the lighter foliage and lichen.

3 Next pin on more berried ivy and lichen. Add largish sprigs of eucalyptus seedpods, which should be long enough to fan out gracefully from the centre to form an outer circle of white. Pin on a little more lichen to the inner edge.

4 Finally, pin on a piece of soft, old rope, roughly 20 cm (8 in) long. Tease it gently so that it curves sinuously through the plant material and buries its ends in the other leaves. Although attached in small sections for ease of handling, the rope should look like one continuous piece when you have finished. When you are satisfied with this section, move on clockwise to your next bare section of wreath, and repeat the procedure from step 2. As a final touch, I also think it is nice to put a knot in the last piece of rope to give the impression that it is anchored in firmly.

WHITE FLOWERS

There is something quiet and ethereal about white flowers. In winter they reflect the cold of the conditions outside and echo a landscape drained of colour. If you are on a tight budget, try grouping together small pretty containers, and inserting a few stems of your favourite flowers in each. Here I have used a collection of delicate phials and vases to display stephanotis, Christmas roses and amaryllis.

FROM LEFT TO RIGHT

Stephanotis, amaryllis, Christmas roses, and arum lillies.

A splash of Christmas colour is easily achieved with red amaryllis heads and red roses, red chilli peppers, anemones, berries and kangaroo paws. Notice that the flowers have been deliberately clustered in their varieties to create more natural groupings. The basket was something I made myself from glycerined magnolia leaves, which I first dyed a deep, dramatic green before simply gluing them on to a low plastic bowl to form an unusual container. I then lined the basket with polythene and floral foam before inserting the flowers. People often think of amaryllis as pot plants, but with their huge trumpet-like flowers they make a tremendous focal point for any arrangement. A few will really go a long way and they last surprisingly well as cut flowers.

A CHRISTMAS SPICE BASKET

Christmas is the time when the home becomes the focus for family and friends. This is a splendid opportunity to indulge any whims or theatrical notions to suit the festive season.

Simple fruit and spices make some of the best Christmas decorations. Here clove-stuckered pomanders, cape gooseberries and sticks of cinnamon fill a wire basket with sweet smells and pretty textures.

METHOD

1 You need to make your glittering pomanders fairly well in advance. Choose largish oranges and insert cloves carefully down the length of each.

2 Wrap a ribbon or piece of decorative gold twine tightly round the pomander so that it crosses in the middle, dividing the orange into eight pieces.

3 Leave the oranges in an airing cupboard to dry completely.

4 At Christmas, display your pomanders with colourful and aromatic fruits and spices, such as bunches of cinnamon sticks, cape gooseberries, tangerines and kumquats.

CHRISTMAS TOPIARY

PREVIOUS PAGE FROM LEFT TO RIGHT
Moss ball, round holly tree, jewelled sphere, tall holly tree, lichen tree.

MOSS BALL
A ball of dry florist's foam is attached to a cane fixed in a pot of plaster of Paris. Soft carpet moss is wrapped round the sphere, and held with gold twine.

JEWELLED SPHERE
Instead of covering the sphere of foam with moss, wire on chilli peppers and add a cluster or two of pepper berries.

TALL HOLLY TREE AND LICHEN TREE
For these two trees, a cone of dry florist's foam forms the shape of the tree and a cinnamon stick the stem. For the holly tree, pin leaves on individually like overlapping slates, starting from the bottom and working up to the top. To cover the final join and top off the tree, add a cluster of berries and leaves. For the lichen tree, pin the moss uniformly all over the cone, using small hairpins of wire. Cover the base with the moss to finish.

As an alternative to floral decorations, topiary trees are always popular at Christmas. Here are five different designs that all rely on strong shapes for their impact. They will also last the whole season.

METHOD: *(Round holly tree)*

1 First select a suitable terracotta pot and a piece of wood or branch to form the trunk. The visible branch needs to be about one and a half times as tall as your container. Fill the pot with some plaster of Paris and insert the stem of the topiary into the centre, leaving the plaster to set firm. Alternatively, you could wedge the branch in some dry florist's foam, although this is not quite as secure as plaster of Paris.

3 To cover the tree you need small pieces of variegated holly, each with two or three leaves. If you can find holly leaves with berries attached, that would look even better! The leaf clusters should all be about the same length to ensure the tree has a strong shape. Wire up each leaf cluster by wrapping florist's wire round the stem. Cut the wire off, leaving two 2.5-cm (1-in) ends of wire exposed to form a hairpin.

2 Next wind some hairy garden string round the upper part of the stem and start winding in small pieces of sphagnum moss. When you have a really nice globe of moss, secure the string and trim away any loose tendrils.

4 Insert each hairpin of holly, starting with a line round the sphere from top to bottom, bisecting this with another line around the diameter (rather like a pomander ribbon). Neatly fill in each section until all your moss is covered.

CANDLELIGHT

What would Christmas be without candles? These tapered sticks of wax hold a magical quality that enchants everyone from the smallest child to the wisest grandmother. Beeswax is one of the prettiest materials for candles, and smells much sweeter than the crude tallow wax which was once used for candlemaking. For Christmas Day itself, you might like to group scented candles together in a sort of still-life display. Decorate the bases with ribbon or wrap leaves sprayed with gold round the candle holders.

Pretty pots of candles are always delightful presents. They are simple to make and won't cost much more than the price of the candle and the terracotta pot. Here I have used gold candles, plunging them into a small pot filled with plaster of Paris. When the plaster sets, the candle is held firm, and you can then cover the surface with decorative moss. As a final touch, a knot of raffia completes the small container.

Larger candles can be decorated with glycerined leaves, shells or glittering ribbons. However, it is very important to take note of fire precautions: make sure your decorations are pushed well down away from the candle flame, and never leave decorated candles burning in an empty room.

LEFT

There are many types of chandelier available today, probably because of the current vogue for wrought iron. Here I have covered the base of the chandelier with moss, before wiring on pots of candles and Christmas roses. For an unashamedly romantic look, you could go a stage further by extending fronds of ivy down from it, and light long elegant tapered candles for the meal itself. Again, never let the candles burn down near the moss or plant materials, and always extinguish them before leaving the room.

FAR LEFT

This free-standing candelabra (opposite) is decorated with strips of dried orange peel and dried mushrooms, which have been tinged with gold paint before being hooked and woven through the frame. The burnt oranges, browns and gold echo the rusty colours of the old frame beautifully.

PREVIOUS PAGE

A selection of Christmas candles, in candlesticks, terracotta pots and artichoke candle holders. To make an artichoke holder, you need to cut the artichoke stem flat to the base so that it will sit on a flat surface. Then carefully hollow out the centre. Paint the artichoke leaves gold and insert a candle into the hollow.

A CHRISTMAS URN

I think that an impressive hall decoration is really worth the effort of making at Christmas, when family gatherings or festive parties demand that the house looks at its best. Large-scale does not necessarily mean expensive, however, and one of the best ways to achieve a generous look without going mad with a cheque book, is to maximize the variety of garden foliage, and also use fruit as focal points. When you analyse this Christmas urn, you can see that for flora I have used only a few stems of amaryllis, a potted cyclamen, and three small winter roses. But the effect is still rich, owing to the presence of less expensive items such as the cascading grapes, the apples and pears burnished with white and gold, and the varied foliage.

METHOD

1 Select a large urn, or pedestal and build up on it four or more blocks of pre-soaked florist's foam, binding them together with florist's tape. Cover this mound with chicken wire.

2 Start your arrangement at the base with the fruit. Take your apples and skewer them each in turn with a sharp stick. Then plunge the sticks into the base of the foam so that the apples sit roughly at the centre of the urn. Add the grapes slightly to the right of the apples, letting them tumble down the urn.

3 Next delineate the outer edges of the complete arrangement with your longest pieces of foliage. If you bear in mind that the display is roughly triangular, this will help you get the right shape. Place your longest stems at either side of the foam block, and then another long stem pointing directly upwards in the centre of

the foam. I used a mixture of camellia branches and lichen-covered larch branches for my triangular shape.

4 Next fill in with blue noble pine, Christmas roses, amaryllis, variegated ivy and eucalyptus. I have also added small pots of cyclamen by pushing a stick through the pots' drainage holes and then into the foam block.

5 Add one or two pieces of skewered fruit higher up and globe artichokes.

6 If you like, you can add a touch of white and gold paint to the fruit. Apply it only to the extremities of the material with a very light touch, to suggest that it has been caught by a cold blast of wind.

7 Finish the arrangement by adding a few long strands of ivy and eucalyptus to reach down over the sides of the urn.

BYZANTINE TONES

Floral gifts are some of the most appreciated presents exchanged at this time of the year. A carefully planted window box full of winter pansies, hebe and ivy would delight anyone living in a flat. A beautiful terrracotta pot planted with a small box tree would be warmly welcomed by a keen gardener, and a basket of planted hyacinth bulbs and moss would find favour with just about anyone.

Here is a slightly more unusual floral gift idea – an arrangement of potted pansies and azaleas interspersed with stems of anemone and roses. The colours are rich and enticing, and the shape of the bowl – shallow and circular – allows you to see the material well from above, making a wide and generous display. A fine piece of heavy brocade is a slightly theatrical touch, which I think enhances the velvety petals of the pansies and roses.

METHOD

1 Once you have selected an appropriate shallow, wide container, you need to find a smaller container that will fit inside it. Fill this with pre-soaked florist's foam, making sure the foam comes up slightly higher than the sides of the inner container but not the outer one. This allows you to insert stems at an upward angle so that the stems droop down. This not only means the arrangement looks more natural, but you can echo the fluid lines of the fabric.

2 Secure the foam with florist's tape. Before you add the flowers, cut a piece of polythene to a size similar to your fabric strip and lay it on top of the foam.

3 Drape your fabric over the polythene so that you can see only exposed foam on either side.

4 Next insert a pot of azaleas by pushing a sharp twig or piece of garden cane through the drainage hole of the pot and then through the foam.

5 Repeat this staking process with three or four small pots of pansies, so that they are each skewered to the foam with a piece of cane. Make sure that you position the pots at an angle so that the arrangement looks quite natural.

6 Cover the pots with delicate grey lichen. This is best pinned in place with small hair-pin shaped pieces of medium-gauge florist's wire. The lichen hides any of the pot edges effectively.

7 Finally, insert a few stems of roses and anemones into the remaining gaps and soften the edges with trails of ivy.

Lavish and aromatic festoons of fruit, flowers and leaves, swags are traditional if not de rigeur at Christmas. They can either hang straight down from a wall or be caught up at both sides to dip and curve like a plump snake from a mantelpiece, staircase or chimney breast. If you are lucky enough to have a decorative fireplace or an impressive banister rail, then a colourful swag will be your most admired Christmas decoration. As swags are quite labour-intensive to prepare, it is best to make one up out of dried material or evergreens so that it will last at least through the main festive week.

CHRISTMAS FABRIC SWAG

Here is a very interesting variation on the normal evergreen swag, constructed around a ream of cream glazed cotton. The browns and creams of the fruit and plant materials make a refreshing change from Christmas colours, and tie in nicely with the ornaments on the fireplace. Although the bows look like part of the length of fabric, they have been added separately and stiffened with pieces of wire glued to their inner lengths.

I always think it is particularly nice to use scented ingredients in a swag, and this one should suffuse a warm room with essences of cinnamon, orange and star anise. Take note of safety precautions too, by making sure that the swag is caught up high enough to avoid any fire hazard.

METHOD

1 First cut out a cardboard template of the shape and size of swag you require - this will be governed by where you want to put it. The cardboard must be fairly sturdy so that it supports the weight of the plant material and the fabric.

2 Lay your card template on a flat surface and cover it with blocks of dry florist's foam, fixed in place with strong tape. Trim the foam to exactly the same size as the template and cover it with chicken wire to give it added strength, again using strong tape to hold in place.

3 Buy a length of cheap cotton, calico or muslin, that will drape nicely. You need about twice the length of your proposed swag, plus about half as much again for the bows. If your fireplace is about 1m (1yd) across, you will need roughly 3m (3yd) of fabric. Find the centre of your swag and pin to the centre of the fabric.

4 Decorate the swag by working from the centre, moving a little to the left and then a little to the right to maintain symmetry. First pin up a section of the fabric, twisting and tucking it as you go. you can use florist's wire to secure it in place, or even long dressmaker's pins. Then pin on small clusters of moss, spices, dried oranges, chestnuts, chilli peppers, lichen, pomegranates and cinnamon sticks. Wind in a piece of gold ribbon as you go.

5 Finally, when you have worked your swag up to both ends, finish it off with two separate fabric bows. Make each of these by cutting a chevron shape out of each end of a strip of calico. Stiffen the fabric by gluing a piece of wire along both edges of the length and folding the fabric around it to form a 1 cm (1/4 in) hem. You can then tie the strip into a generous bow, which holds its shape.

GLOSSARY

Acacia dealbata MIMOSA
COLOUR: *Yellow flowers, blue-green leaves.*
AVAILABILITY: *Spring.*
LIFESPAN: *Approximately five days.*
CARE: *Trim stems and remove lower foliage.*

Aconitum MONKSHOOD
COLOUR: *blue, lilac or white hood-like flowers.*
AVAILABILITY: *Summer and autumn.*
LIFESPAN: *Approximately ten days.*
CARE: *Trim stems and remove lower foliage. They can be easily dried by suspending in a warm, dry environment. The roots are extremely poisonous so handle with care.*

Alcea HOLLYHOCK
COLOUR: *White, red, yellow, orange, pink.*
AVAILABILITY: *Summer.*
LIFESPAN: *Approximately one week.*
CARE: *Trim stems, remove lower foliage and stand in deep water.*

Alchemilla mollis LADY'S MANTLE
COLOUR: *Scalloped green leaves and lime-green flowers.*
AVAILABILITY: *Early summer to autumn.*
LIFESPAN: *Approximately one week.*
CARE: *Remove lower foliage. They can easily be dried by suspending in a warm, dry environment.*

Alstroemeria PERUVIAN LILY
COLOUR: *Pink, orange, yellow, red.*
AVAILABILITY: *Summer.*
LIFESPAN: *Approximately two weeks.*

CARE: *Trim stems and remove lower foliage. Buy when flowers are just beginning to show colour. Remove wilted flowers, as this will encourage more buds to open.*

Amaranthus LOVE-LIES-BLEEDING
COLOUR: *Red, green.*
AVAILABILITY: *Summer and autumn.*
LIFESPAN: *Two weeks.*
CARE: *Trim stems and remove foliage. They can easily be dried by suspending in a warm, dry environment.*

Anemone WINDFLOWER
COLOUR: *White, pink, purple, red, blue.*
AVAILABILITY: *Spring or autumn.*
LIFESPAN: *Some varieties last only a few days, others are much longer lasting.*
CARE: *Cut the stems and put in water as soon as possible.*

Anthurium
COLOUR: *White, green, red.*
AVAILABILITY: *All year round.*
LIFESPAN: *Approximately one month.*
CARE: *Trim stems; take care not to bruise the petals.*

Antirrhinum SNAPDRAGON
COLOUR: *Most, except blue.*
AVAILABILITY: *Summer; all year round commercially.*
LIFESPAN: *Approximately five to seven days.*
CARE: *Cut stems and remove lower foliage. Remove flowers as they wilt to encourage new buds to open.*

Aquilegia COLUMBINE
COLOUR: *Red, yellow, blue, white, pink, purple; some varieties are bi-coloured.*
AVAILABILITY: *Summer.*
LIFESPAN: *Two to three days.*
CARE: *Trim stems. They need plenty of water.*

Aster MICHAELMAS DAISY
COLOUR: *White, yellow, lavender-blue, pink, red.*
AVAILABILITY: *Late summer to autumn.*
LIFESPAN: *Five to eight days.*
CARE: *Trim stems and remove the foliage as this tends to deteriorate very quickly.*

Buddleja BUTTERFLY BUSH
COLOUR: *Purple, white, lilac, yellow, orange.*
AVAILABILITY: *Summer.*
LIFESPAN: *Approximately five days.*
CARE: *Trim stems at a sharp angle and stand in deep water before arranging.*

Calendula MARIGOLD
COLOUR: *Orange, yellow.*
AVAILABILITY: *Summer, but generally available from florists all year round.*
LIFESPAN: *Approximately one week.*
CARE: *Trim stems and remove lower leaves.*

Camellia
COLOUR: *White, pink, peach, red, purple.*
AVAILABILITY: *Flowers in spring, foliage all year.*
LIFESPAN: *Flowers one week; foliage three weeks.*
CARE: *Trim stems. The open flowers are easily damaged so arrange very carefully.*

Capsicum SWEET PEPPER
COLOUR: *Red, yellow, orange, green.*
AVAILABILITY: *Autumn.*
LIFESPAN: *They last very well, even without water.*
CARE: *Trim woody stems before placing in water. They can also be used dry in an arrangement.*

Ceanothus CALIFORNIAN LILAC
COLOUR: *Several shades of blue.*
AVAILABILITY: *Most flower in spring, some in summer and early autumn.*
LIFESPAN: *Approximately two weeks.*
CARE: *Cut woody stems and remove lower foliage.*

Centaurea CORNFLOWER
COLOUR: *Blue, pink, red, purple, white.*
AVAILABILITY: *Summer.*
LIFESPAN: *Approximately one week.*
CARE: *Trim the stems at a sharp angle and remove any foliage below the water-line.*

Choisya ternata MEXICAN ORANGE BLOSSOM
COLOUR: *White flowers, glossy green foliage.*
AVAILABILITY: *Foliage all year round; flowers in spring and autumn.*
LIFESPAN: *Approximately two weeks.*
CARE: *Cut stems at a sharp angle and remove foliage below the water-line.*

Chrysanthemum
COLOUR: *Most are available.*
AVAILABILITY: *Autumn; commercially all year round.*
LIFESPAN: *From one to three weeks depending on variety.*
CARE: *Trim stems at a sharp angle and remove any foliage below the water-line.*

Clivia **KAFFIR LILY**
COLOUR: *Red, orange, yellow.*
AVAILABILITY: *Spring and summer.*
LIFESPAN: *Approximately two weeks.*
CARE: *Trim stems and stand in deep water for several hours before arranging.*

Cornus alba **DOGWOOD**
COLOUR: *Red or yellow bark; yellow or white flowers; black or red fruits.*
AVAILABILITY: *Bark in winter; flowers in spring and autumn; fruit in autumn.*
LIFESPAN: *Very long lasting.*
CARE: *Trim stems.*

Cotoneaster
COLOUR: *Red, black, orange or yellow berries; white or pink flowers.*
AVAILABILITY: *Flowers in spring, berries in autumn.*
LIFESPAN: *Approximately two to three weeks.*
CARE: *Cut stems at sharp angles and remove any foliage or berries below the water-line. It can sometimes look rather stiff, so mix with something softer such as ivy.*

Cytisus **BROOM**
COLOUR: *Yellow, red, white, pink, cream, or bi-coloured. C.battandieri has large silvery leaves and dense spikes of yellow flowers smelling of pineapple.*
AVAILABILITY: *Flowers in spring and early summer.*
LIFESPAN: *Flowers about one week; foliage about two weeks.*
CARE: *Cut stems at a sharp angle.*

Dahlia
COLOUR: *Every colour except blue.*
AVAILABILITY: *Late summer and autumn.*
LIFESPAN: *From one week to ten days.*

CARE: *Stand in deep water for several hours before arranging. Avoid knocking the heads as the flowers tend to shatter very easily.*

Delphinium
COLOUR: *Blue, white, cream, grey, pink.*
AVAILABILITY: *Flowers in summer, but available commercially all year round.*
LIFESPAN: *Approximately one week.*
CARE: *Some of the larger blooms may have weak stems which can be supported with a piece of cane. Dry by suspending in a warm environment.*

Dianthus **CARNATION, PINK**
COLOUR: *Pink, peach, white, red, purple, or bi-coloured.*
AVAILABILITY: *Summer; all year round from florists.*
LIFESPAN: *Approximately one week.*
CARE: *Buy before the central white stamens show.*

Digitalis **FOXGLOVE**
COLOUR: *White, purple, red, pink, yellow, peach.*
AVAILABILITY: *Summer.*
LIFESPAN: *Approximately six days.*
CARE: *Trim stems and remove lower foliage. Always bear in mind that this is a poisonous plant.*

Echinops **GLOBE THISTLE**
COLOUR: *Blue flowers, grey-white foliage.*
AVAILABILITY: *Summer; all year round from florists.*
LIFESPAN: *Long lasting in water; dries easily.*
CARE: *Stand in deep water for several hours before arranging; dry by suspending them in a warm, dry environment.*

Erica **HEATHER**
COLOUR: *Purple, pink, white, peach, gold.*
AVAILABILITY: *All year round.*
LIFESPAN: *Long lasting when cut.*
CARE: *Trim woody stems and remove lower foliage and florets. Dry in a vase without water.*

Eryngium **SEA HOLLY**
COLOUR: *Blue, green.*
AVAILABILITY: *Summer and autumn.*
LIFESPAN: *Long lasting.*
CARE: *Stand in deep water before arranging. Dry by suspending them in a warm, dry environment.*

Euphorbia **SPURGE**
COLOUR: *Yellow, red, orange-red flowers.*
AVAILABILITY: *Spring and summer; winter for greenhouse varieties.*
LIFESPAN: *Approximately two weeks.*
CARE: *Stand in deep water for several hours before arranging. Handle with care as the white sap can cause irritation.*

Eustoma **LISIANTHUS**
COLOUR: *White, cream, pink, lilac, purple; bi-coloured.*
AVAILABILITY: *Summer, but now generally available throughout the year.*
LIFESPAN: *Approximately one week.*
CARE: *Stand in deep water for several hours before arranging. Buds often wilt; if this is the case, trim stems, wrap in newspaper, and stand upright in deep water.*

Forsythia
COLOUR: *Yellow.*
AVAILABILITY: *Spring.*
LIFESPAN: *Approximately one week.*
CARE: *Cut stems at a sharp angle and remove flowers below the water-line. If the effect looks rather stiff, gently bend the forsythia branches when arranging.*

Freesia
COLOUR: *White, yellow, pink, mauve, red. The yellow varieties in particular have a fine fragrance.*
AVAILABILITY: *Winter and spring; all year from florists, usually in mixed colours, but they have recently become available in single colours.*
LIFESPAN: *Approximately seven to ten days.*
CARE: *Trim stems and stand in water.*

Gardenia
COLOUR: *White.*
AVAILABILITY: *All year round as pot plants. It is now very difficult to buy them as cut flowers commercially in this country.*
LIFESPAN: *Long lasting.*
CARE: *Cut stems at a sharp angle and place in water. Avoid bruising the petals.*

Garrya **TASSEL BUSH**
COLOUR: *Green-grey catkins.*

AVAILABILITY: *Catkins in winter and early spring.*
LIFESPAN: *Approximately two to three weeks.*
CARE: *Cut stems at a sharp angle and remove foliage below the water-line.*

Gladiolus **SWORD LILY**
COLOUR: *Most colours, except blue.*
AVAILABILITY: *Summer and autumn.*
LIFESPAN: *Ten days to two weeks.*
CARE: *Trim stems at a sharp angle. Remove any dead blooms from the base to encourage new buds to open.*

Gypsophila
COLOUR: *White, pink.*
AVAILABILITY: *Summer.*
LIFESPAN: *Long lasting. They can also be easily dried.*
CARE: *Stand in deep water for several hours before arranging. Always buy when the flowers are in bloom as the green buds rarely open.*

Hebe **SHRUBBY VERONICA**
COLOUR: *White, pink or blue flowers. There are some attractive variegated forms*
AVAILABILITY: *Flowers in summer and autumn; foliage all year round.*
LIFESPAN: *Approximately two weeks.*
CARE: *Trim stems at a sharp angle and remove lower leaves.*

Hedera **IVY**
COLOUR: *Green or variegated leaves.*
AVAILABILITY: *All year round.*
LIFESPAN: *Approximately two to three weeks.*
CARE: *Trim stems and remove leaves below the water-line.*

Helianthus **SUNFLOWER**
COLOUR: *Yellow daisy-like flowers with a distinctive brown centre.*
AVAILABILITY: *Summer and autumn.*
LIFESPAN: *Approximately one week in water.*
CARE: *Trim stems at a sharp angle and stand in deep water. If the petals are bruised or damaged, remove them and use the seed heads on their own.*

Helichrysum **STRAWFLOWER**
COLOUR: *Yellow, white, pink, purple, red or brown daisy-like flowers with a papery texture.*

AVAILABILITY: *Summer.*
LIFESPAN: *Very long lasting.*
CARE: *Stand in deep water for several hours before arranging. Dry by suspending in a warm, dry environment.*

Helleborus **CHRISTMAS ROSE, LENTEN ROSE**
COLOUR: *White, green, plum or pink disc-shaped flowers with golden or green stamens. Some are spotted.*
AVAILABILITY: *Winter and spring.*
LIFESPAN: *Long lasting.*
CARE: *Trim stems at a sharp angle and plunge immediately into water.*

Hosta **PLANTAIN LILY**
Large, heart-shaped leaves available in many different sizes and colours, including some variegated forms. This is a wonderful foliage plant but the arching, bell-shaped flowers are also worthy of a place in many summer arrangements. Use grouped low in displays .
COLOUR: *Green, yellow or blue-grey heart-shaped leaves; white, blue or mauve flowers.*
AVAILABILITY: *Summer and autumn.*
LIFESPAN: *Approximately two weeks.*
CARE: *Trim stems at a sharp angle.*

Hyacinthus **HYACINTH**
COLOUR: *Blue, white, pink, yellow.*
AVAILABILITY: *Spring.*
LIFESPAN: *Approximately ten days as a cut flower.*
CARE: *Cut stems close to the bulb for maximum stem length. Wash sap away under running water before arranging.*

Hydrangea
COLOUR: *Blue, mauve, white, pink.*
AVAILABILITY: *Summer and autumn.*
LIFESPAN: *Approximately one week.*
CARE: *Cut stems at a sharp angle and stand in deep water for several hours before arranging. If the flowers wilt, wrap in newspaper and stand upright in deep water.*

Ilex **HOLLY**
COLOUR: *Green or variegated leaves; red or yellow berries.*

AVAILABILITY: *Foliage all year round; bright red berries in winter.*
LIFESPAN: *Can last for several weeks depending on variety.*
CARE: *Trim stems at a sharp angle.*

Iris
COLOUR: *White, blue, purple, yellow.*
AVAILABILITY: *From the delicate dwarf varieties to the tall summer-flowering varieties there is an iris for virtually every month of the year.*
LIFESPAN: *Approximately one week.*
CARE: *Trim stems at a sharp angle.*

Jasminum **JASMINE**
COLOUR: *Yellow, white or pink star-shaped flowers.*
AVAILABILITY: *Summer, winter.*
LIFESPAN: *Long lasting, especially the winter forms.*
CARE: *Trim stems at a sharp angle and stand in deep water for several hours before you begin to arrange.*

Lathyrus **SWEET PEA**
COLOUR: *Pink, blue, purple, white, lilac, cream, red, peach; many are bi-coloured.*
AVAILABILITY: *Summer and early autumn.*
LIFESPAN: *Approximately five to eight days.*
CARE: *Trim stems. Stand in a cool environment and do not allow the petals to become damp.*

Lavandula **LAVENDER**
COLOUR: *Lavender-blue; there are also pink and white varieties.*
AVAILABILITY: *Summer and autumn.*
LIFESPAN: *Approximately two weeks. Can also be dried.*
CARE: *Stand in deep water for several hours before arranging. Dry by suspending in a dry environment.*

Lavatera **MALLOW**
COLOUR: *Purple, pink or white trumpet-shaped flowers.*
AVAILABILITY: *Summer.*
LIFESPAN: *Approximately ten days.*
CARE: *Trim stems at a sharp angle; remove any dead flower heads to encourage new buds start to open.*

Liatris **GAY FEATHERS**
Clump-forming perennials with grass-like foliage and tall spikes of feathery purple flowers. Part of their appeal lies in the fact that the flowers open from the top down.
COLOUR: *Purple.*
AVAILABILITY: *Summer; all year round commercially.*
LIFESPAN: *Long lasting.*
CARE: *Trim stems and remove foliage below the water-line.*

Lilium **LILY**
COLOUR: *Most, except blue.*
AVAILABILITY: *Summer and autumn; all year round commercially.*
LIFESPAN: *Approximately three weeks.*
CARE: *Trim stems at a sharp angle and remove foliage below the water-line. It is advisable to remove the stamens as the pollen will stain.*

Limonium **SEA LAVENDER, STATICE**
COLOUR: *Blue, yellow, pink, purple, white.*
AVAILABILITY: *Summer and autumn; all year round from florists.*
LIFESPAN: *Very long lasting when dried.*
CARE: *Trim stems. Dry by suspending in a warm environment.*

Lonicera **HONEYSUCKLE**
COLOUR: *White, yellow, orange, red.*
AVAILABILITY: *Summer and autumn.*
LIFESPAN: *Approximately one week for flowers in bud form.*
CARE: *Trim stems at a sharp angle and stand in deep water for several hours before arranging.*

Lunaria **HONESTY**
COLOUR: *Pink, white, purple; silver seed pods.*
AVAILABILITY: *Flowers in summer; seed pods in autumn.*
LIFESPAN: *Flowers approximately one week; seed pods can be dried.*
CARE: *Trim stems before arranging. To dry, suspend in a warm environment for about one week.*

Lupinus **LUPIN**
COLOUR: *Yellow, orange-red, blue, pink, white, purple florets.*

AVAILABILITY: *Summer.*
LIFESPAN: *Approximately one week.*
CARE: *Trim stems at a sharp angle, remove lower foliage, and stand in deep water for several hours before arranging.*

Lysimachia **YELLOW LOOSESTRIFE**
COLOUR: *Yellow, red, grey, white.*
AVAILABILITY: *Summer.*
LIFESPAN: *Approximately four to seven days.*
CARE: *Trim stems at a sharp angle, remove leaves from below the water-line, and place in deep water for several hours before starting to arrange.*

Magnolia
COLOUR: *Cream, white, pink, or purple waxy flowers.*
AVAILABILITY: *Spring and summer.*
LIFESPAN: *Approximately two weeks.*
CARE: *Stand in deep water for several hours before arranging. Handle with care as the flower heads can be very easily damaged.*

Malope
COLOUR: *Pink, purple, white.*
availability: *Summer and early autumn.*
LIFESPAN: *Long lasting.*
CARE: *Cut stems at a sharp angle, remove foliage from lower stem, and place in deep water for several hours before arranging.*

Mahonia
COLOUR: *Yellow bell-shaped flowers. Dusky purple berries are produced in late spring and the leaves turn burnt red in autumn.*
AVAILABILITY: *Flowers from late autumn to spring; foliage all year round.*
LIFESPAN: *Flowers approximately one week, foliage three weeks.*
CARE: *Trim stems at a sharp angle. The leaves can be exceptionally thorny so handle with care when arranging.*

Matthiola **STOCK**
COLOUR: *Purple, pink, red, yellow, white, cream.*
AVAILABILITY: *Summer.*
LIFESPAN: *Approximately one week.*
CARE: *Trim stems and stand in deep water for several hours before arranging.*

Muscari **GRAPE HYACINTH**
Spring-flowering bulbous plants with bright green, leafless stems, bearing dense spikes of small blue or white flowers.
COLOUR: *Blue, white.*
AVAILABILITY: *Winter and spring.*
LIFESPAN: *Approximately one week.*
CARE: *Trim a tiny amount from the stems.*

Narcissus **DAFFODIL**
COLOUR: *Yellow, white, cream, apricot or orange trumpet-shaped flowers.*
AVAILABILITY: *Spring; winter and spring commercially.*
LIFESPAN: *Some varieties last only a few days, others are very long lasting. Also use pots of daffodils in container displays. These should last several weeks.*
CARE: *Trim stems and stand in deep water for several hours before arranging.*

Nepeta **CATMINT**
COLOUR: *Lavender-blue flowers; grey-green foliage.*
AVAILABILITY: *Summer.*
LIFESPAN: *Approximately two weeks.*
CARE: *Trim stems and remove lower foliage before arranging.*

Nerine
COLOUR: *Pink, white, red.*
AVAILABILITY: *Autumn.*
LIFESPAN: *Approximately two weeks.*
CARE: *Trim stems before arranging.*

Nicotiana TOBACCO PLANT
COLOUR: *Red, yellow, white, pink, and green;*
AVAILABILITY: *Summer and autumn.*
LIFESPAN: *Only a couple of days as a cut flower.*
CARE: *Cut stems and place in water for several hours before arranging.*

Nigella LOVE-IN-A-MIST
COLOUR: *Blue, white or pink flowers.*
AVAILABILITY: *Summer.*
LIFESPAN: *Approximately two weeks.*
CARE: *Trim stems and remove lower foliage before arranging. Dry by suspending in a warm environment.*

Orchid
COLOUR: *White, pink, green, purple, apricot, brown.*
AVAILABILITY: *All year round.*
LIFESPAN: *Approximately three weeks.*
CARE: *Trim stems.*

Osteospermum
COLOUR: *Pink, yellow, white.*
AVAILABILITY: *Summer and autumn.*
LIFESPAN: *Approximately five days.*
CARE: *Trim stems.*

Paeonia PEONY
COLOUR: *White, pink, red.*
AVAILABILITY: *Summer.*
LIFESPAN: *Approximately one week.*
CARE: *Trim stems at a sharp angle and remove foliage below the water-line.*

Papaver POPPY
COLOUR: *Pink, red, cream, apricot, white, orange, purple.*
AVAILABILITY: *Summer and autumn.*
LIFESPAN: *Approximately one to five days, depending on variety; seed heads indefinitely*
CARE: *they should be cut just as the buds open. The seed heads can be dried by suspending in a warm environment.*

Pelargonium GERANIUM
COLOUR: *Pink, red, purple, white, peach.*
AVAILABILITY: *Summer and autumn flowering.*
LIFESPAN: *As cut flowers approximately five days*
CARE: *Trim stems at an angle.*

Philadelphus MOCK ORANGE
COLOUR: *White or cream cup-shaped flowers and papery green leaves.*
AVAILABILITY: *Summer.*
LIFESPAN: *Approximately one week.*
CARE: *Trim stems at an angle, and place in deep water immediately after cutting as sometimes prone to wilt.*

Phlox
COLOUR: *Pink, white, mauve.*
AVAILABILITY: *Summer.*
LIFESPAN: *Approximately five days.*
CARE: *Trim stems at an angle and remove foliage below the water-line.*

Physalis CHINESE LANTERN
COLOUR: *White flowers, red calyces, orange fruit.*
AVAILABILITY: *Flowers in summer; calyces and fruit in autumn.*
LIFESPAN: *Long lasting.*
CARE: *Trim stems and remove leaves, as these wilt very quickly. To dry, cut the stems when the calyces are just beginning to colour and then suspend by hanging upside down in a warm environment.*

Polygonatum SOLOMON'S SEAL
COLOUR: *White bell-shaped flowers.*
AVAILABILITY: *Spring.*
LIFESPAN: *Approximately one week.*
CARE: *Trim stems at a sharp angle before standing in water.*

Primula PRIMROSE, POLYANTHUS
COLOUR: *Flowers of almost every colour.*
AVAILABILITY: *Spring and summer.*
LIFESPAN: *Approximately four days.*
CARE: *Stand in deep water for several hours before arranging. Handle with care as the fine hairs on the foliage can sometimes cause skin irritation.*

Protea
COLOUR: *Pink, green, white, grey.*
AVAILABILITY: *All year round.*
LIFESPAN: *Approximately one month.*
CARE: *Using a sharp knife carefully trim the woody stems. Dry by suspending in a warm environment.*

Prunus CHERRY
COLOUR: *Pink or white single or double flowers.*
AVAILABILITY: *Spring.*
LIFESPAN: *Approximately one week.*
CARE: *Carefully trim stems with a sharp knife at an angle.*

Rhododendron
COLOUR: *White, apricot, purple, pink, red, yellow.*
AVAILABILITY: *Flowers in spring.*
LIFESPAN: *Approximately seven days in flower, two to three weeks as foliage.*
CARE: *Trim woody stems at a sharp angle and remove foliage below the water-line.*

Rosa ROSE
COLOUR: *Shades of practically every colour.*
AVAILABILITY: *All year round.*
LIFESPAN: *From about five days to two weeks depending on variety.*
CARE: *They are best cut when in bud. Trim stems at a sharp angle and remove thorns. Stand in deep water for several hours before arranging.*

Rosmarinus ROSEMARY
COLOUR: *Grey-green foliage and blue, white or pink flowers.*
AVAILABILITY: *Foliage all year round; flowers in spring and autumn.*
LIFESPAN: *Approximately two weeks.*
CARE: *Trim woody stems at a sharp angle, and remove foliage below the water-line.*

Rubus **BRAMBLE**
COLOUR: *Pink or white flowers.*
AVAILABILITY: *Autumn.*
CARE: *Trim stems and remove thorns.*

Rudbeckia **CONEFLOWER**
COLOUR: *Yellow or orange daisy-like flowers.*
AVAILABILITY: *Late summer to autumn.*
LIFESPAN: *Approximately two weeks.*
CARE: *Trim stems at a sharp angle, remove foliage below the water-line, and place in deep water for several hours before arranging.*

Salix **WILLOW**
COLOUR: *Stems in a wide range of colours; catkins yellow.*
AVAILABILITY: *Stems in winter; catkins in spring.*
LIFESPAN: *Long lasting in water where the buds will continue to develop and shoot into leaf.*
CARE: *Cut stems at a sharp angle.*

Scabiosa **SCABIOUS**
COLOUR: *Pale blue, lilac, pink.*
AVAILABILITY: *Summer.*
LIFESPAN: *Approximately six days.*
CARE: *Trim stems and stand in deep water for several hours.*

Sedum **ICE PLANT**
COLOUR: *Pink, white, red.*
AVAILABILITY: *Flowers, late summer and autumn; foliage, all year round.*
LIFESPAN: *Two to three weeks.*
CARE: *Trim stems at a sharp angle and remove fleshy leaves from below the water-line.*

Senecio **RAGWORT, CINERARIA**
COLOUR: *Grey-green leaves, yellow or magenta flowers.*
AVAILABILITY: *All year round.*
LIFESPAN: *Approximately two weeks.*
CARE: *Trim stems at a sharp angle and remove leaves below the water-line.*

Skimmia
COLOUR: *White flowers, red berries.*
AVAILABILITY: *Flowers in spring; berries autumn to spring; foliage all year round.*
LIFESPAN: *approximately two weeks.*
CARE: *Trim woody stems at a sharp angle.*

Solidago **GOLDEN ROD**
COLOUR: *Yellow feather-like plumes.*
AVAILABILITY: *Late summer and autumn.*
LIFESPAN: *Approximately five to seven days.*
CARE: *Trim stems and remove foliage beneath the water-line.*

Sorbus **WHITEBEAM**
COLOUR: *White flowers, silver foliage, orange-red berries.*
AVAILABILITY: *Flowers in spring; berries in autumn; foliage summer and autumn.*
LIFESPAN: *approximately two weeks.*
CARE: *Trim woody stems at a sharp angle and remove foliage beneath the water-line.*

Spiraea
COLOUR: *White, pink flowers.*
AVAILABILITY: *Spring and early summer.*
LIFESPAN: *Approximately one week.*
CARE: *Trim stems and remove lower foliage.*

Stachys **LAMB'S EARS**
COLOUR: *Pink flowers, silver-grey leaves.*
AVAILABILITY: *Summer and autumn.*
LIFESPAN: *One week to ten days.*
CARE: *Trim stems. The velvety coating of the leaves can easily be damaged by water.*

Stephanotis **WAX FLOWER**
COLOUR: *White.*
AVAILABILITY: *Flowers spring to autumn; all year round from florists.*
LIFESPAN: *Approximately ten days as a cut flower.*
CARE: *Trim stems and stand in water.*

Syringa **LILAC**
COLOUR: *Shades of mauve, purple, pink, white.*
AVAILABILITY: *Spring.*
LIFESPAN: *Approximately ten days.*
CARE: *Trim stems at a sharp angle and stand in deep water.*

Thymus **THYME**
COLOUR: *Purple, mauve, white, pink, lilac.*
AVAILABILITY: *Summer.*
LIFESPAN: *Approximately five days.*
CARE: *Trim stems at an angle and remove foliage below the water-line.*

Trachelium
COLOUR: *White, lilac or purple tubular flowers.*
AVAILABILITY: *Spring to autumn.*
LIFESPAN: *Approximately one week.*
CARE: *Trim stems and lower leaves.*

Tulipa **TULIP**
COLOUR: *Shades of practically every colour.*
AVAILABILITY: *Winter and spring commercially.*
LIFESPAN: *Approximately nine days in water.*
CARE: *Trim stems and stand in deep water for several hours.*

Viburnum
COLOUR: *Pink, cream or white flowers; red, black or blue berries.*
AVAILABILITY: *All year round.*
LIFESPAN: *Two weeks.*
CARE: *Trim stems at a sharp angle.*

Viola **VIOLET, PANSY**
COLOUR: *Purple, yellow, white, blue; some are bi-coloured.*
AVAILABILITY: *Spring and summer.*
LIFESPAN: *Approximately five days.*
CARE: *Stand in deep water for several hours before arranging. To resuscitate wilted flowers, submerge completely in water for several hours.*

Xeranthemum **IMMORTELLE**
COLOUR: *Purple, pink or white daisy-like, papery flowers.*
AVAILABILITY: *Summer.*
LIFESPAN: *Approximately one week.*
CARE: *Trim stems and stand in water. Dry by suspending in a warm environment.*

Zantedeschia **ARUM LILY**
COLOUR: *White.*
AVAILABILITY: *Spring and early summer.*
LIFESPAN: *Approximately ten days.*
CARE: *Trim the stems and stand in deep water for several hours before arranging.*

Zinnia
COLOUR: *White, yellow, pink, orange, purple.*
AVAILABILITY: *Summer and autumn.*
LIFESPAN: *Approximately nine days.*
CARE: *It is important to change the water every day as the stems deteriorate very quickly.*

INDEX

P U B L I S H E R ' S   A C K N O W L E D G E M E N T S

The publisher would like to thank the following for lending props for the photography: Anthony Stern Glass, Unit 205, Avro House, Havelock Terrace, London SW8 (for generously loaning his hand-blown glass vases); Antiques & Things, 91 Eccles Road, London SW11; The Dining Room Shop, 62-64 White Hart Lane, London SW13; Angelic Candle Shop, 194 Kings Road, London SW3; V.V Rouleaux, 201 New Kings Road, London SW6; The Conran Shop, Michelin House, 81 Fulham Road, London SW3.
With special thanks to Caroline Taylor, Caroline Taverne and Barbara Mellor for their expert and speedy editorial help.
Index compiled by Indexing Specialists, Hove, East Sussex BN3 2DJ.